14 Days in the Niger Delta

14 Days in the Niger Delta

BY Richard D. AND Stephanie A. Tarpey

RESOURCE *Publications* · Eugene, Oregon

14 DAYS IN THE NIGER DELTA

Resource Publications
An Imprint of Wipf and Stock Publishers
199 W. 8th Ave., Suite 3
Eugene, OR 97401

www.wipfandstock.com

PAPERBACK ISBN: 979-8-3852-0097-9
HARDCOVER ISBN: 979-8-3852-0098-6
EBOOK ISBN: 979-8-3852-0099-3

VERSION NUMBER 12/12/23

Disclaimer

This work is an actual and factual account of events that occurred in the autumn of 2011. The following is from the recollections of my husband and myself. Other people involved have their own viewpoints, which may differ from ours in certain aspects, but this is our story from how we remember it. Conversations have been recreated from our memories. The names and details of some individuals have been changed to respect their privacy.

Dedication

First and foremost, we dedicate this book to God, our Lord Jesus Christ, who brought us through the darkness into the light and without whom none of this would be possible. Thank you to our sons, Rich and Ray, parents, Ray and Joy, sister, Darla, and brother-in-law, Daniel, for your love and support and for living through all of this with us. Thank you, Kathy, for always lifting me up and being my personal counselor. Thank you to our family and friends who prayed for us and supported us then and now. I am so thankful that God has brought all of you into our lives.

Contents

Chapter 1

It's a good thing we don't know the future—we wouldn't want to go past today if we did. Life isn't easy, and everyone has ups and downs, times when everything seems to be running smoothly, and times when nothing seems to go right. Those aren't the times I'm talking about. I am talking about events in our lives that are so dark that we live in a tunnel of fear, unable to lift our heads and look around. Events we have no control over churn us up and spit us out into the void. There have been times when I would have just sat down and refused to go any further if I had known what was coming. The following account is one of those times.

My husband, Richard Tarpey, is a maritime captain. He had been captaining crew boats out of Texas for several years when he started looking into upgrading his captain's license to 1600 tons. The upgrade would give him a broader range of job opportunities with larger companies. We talked about it for months and prayed over the situation because it would mean he would have to quit his job and pay for the classes needed for the upgrade and testing. He already had the maritime hours he needed—but looking at six months of no pay and withdrawing from the company's 401k were big decisions. Finally, after months of discussion and prayer, we came to a conclusion, and Rich handed in his resignation. He enrolled in the classes and had to travel to maritime schools in different states to take the required courses, which was an added expense.

During his last class in Louisiana and testing for his upgrade, Rich met another captain who worked for an offshore oil company in their Nigeria division. The man recommended he go apply, saying that they needed captains—the oil fields offshore of Nigeria were booming. I told him I was worried about piracy when Rich brought it up. There had been a lot in the news

about Somalia and pirates off the coast hijacking ships and kidnapping or shooting crew members, so I voiced my concerns. Still, Rich assured me that the crews were protected in Nigeria and that each boat had military escorts in and out of the ports and rivers. With the loss of pay and the expense of the classes, Rich was worried about getting back to work quickly, so as soon as he completed the course and passed the exams for his license, he drove to the offshore oil company recommended by the other captain in his class and applied for a position as a captain.

He was immediately offered a spot in the Nigeria division. The company's doctor did a physical, and Rich started all the vaccinations and required antimalarial medication he needed to work in Nigeria. He came home for about a week, which passed in a whirlwind of preparation for his trip. He would be a captain on the crew boat for two months and then return home for a month. It was a change from his last work schedule: work for twenty-eight days and then home for fourteen. It was also a substantial raise, and all his travel days were paid. The new timetable was a huge adjustment for our family life. We had not been apart for that amount of time for years. I knew it would be hard to deal with the loneliness and the responsibilities at home alone for two or more months at a time.

To my husband, this new position was just another adventure. Triple black diamond skiing, surfing, sailing for a year with his stepfather, living in Costa Rica and running a ponga boat, skydiving, mountain biking, and offshore fishing were all part of his life history when I met him. Rich had changed a lot during our marriage. He had grown up and taken on the responsibility of a husband, father, and support for the family. God had brought him through alcohol and drug addiction, and he had rededicated his life. He and our youngest son were baptized together. He valued his life with our boys and me and worked hard to support us and further his career. Having him gone so much was not easy, and trying to keep up with everything was complicated, but it was worth it. After everything we had been through during the first four years of our marriage, I prayed for God's will in our lives and for Him to give me the strength to do whatever I needed to raise our sons and keep our family together.

Rich was excited to start his new position. He knew the job's demands since he had been running crew boats for several years. Still, Rich had never worked running supply boats in another country, and he was nervous about what to expect. I was worried about his safety and dealing with everything at home. I knew that if there was an emergency when he was working in

the Gulf of Mexico, his company would replace him, and he could get home quickly. No way could that happen with him in Nigeria. Getting a replacement there would be more complex, and reaching us would take more than a day or two. He gave me all the emergency contact numbers for his supervisors because it would be difficult to call him there.

The boys and I took Rich to the airport, and I cried on the way home after dropping him off. The first three weeks he was at work passed quickly. The boys and I were used to him being gone for three to four weeks at a time, but as the days without Daddy continued, the boys began asking when he would be home. I set up a calendar so they could mark off each day that passed until he was due back. I tried not to stress out over having to make all of the decisions, keeping up with everything at work, making sure the boys made it to school and all their sporting activities, taking care of our pets, and feeling like a single parent, but I wasn't always successful.

The first time I picked Rich up from the airport after his two-month hitch in Nigeria, he hugged me tightly as if he couldn't let me go. As we drove home, the boys peppered him with questions: "Is it hotter than it is here? Did you see any wild animals, like elephants or lions? What is the boat like? What are the people like on your boat?" "Let your dad rest a little bit," I told them. "It's been a really long flight for him, and he hasn't slept for a couple of days, so we should let him get a good night's sleep before we wear him out with questions." They stopped quizzing him and instead began telling him about school and their friends. They helped him carry his luggage into the house when we got home. Our border collie, Lady, and yellow Lab, Sis, began jumping up on him, barking excitedly, and smelling his suitcases. Rich went in to shower and rinse off all the travel smells. I took the boys out to shoot baskets. When Rich finished showering, we ordered pizza since he hadn't eaten it in a couple of months. After we ate, he went to bed, falling into an exhausted sleep. I watched his face relax as he lay there, and I thanked God for bringing him home safely.

In the morning, we talked before the boys woke up. We hadn't really been able to have a conversation about what his new job was like while he was on the boat. He didn't have a strong cell phone signal offshore, and there were usually other crewmembers around when he could call me. It was difficult for Rich, being so far from home and unable to talk with the boys or me each day, so he bought a satellite phone that he had seen other captains use to reach their families even when they were offshore.

The living conditions of the Nigerian people shocked Rich. He said that some of the oil company workers he met on the plane told him the millions of dollars the country made from their offshore oil fields were being paid to the highest government officials. Instead of improving the living conditions of the people and putting money into health and education, they were pocketing the money for their own personal use. The economic gap between the rich and the poor caused a lot of political unrest and a rise in militant groups. He explained what he had seen, his voice filled with disbelief and pain, "When I got off the plane in Lagos, the company officials got me through customs and into a bulletproof car. As we drove to the coast, I saw people lying on the side of the road like you might see an animal on the side of the road here at home that had been hit by a car. These people were dying of starvation or already dead, and everyone just went about their own business like it was nothing. Those people's lives meant less than an animal's life."

When Rich got to the crew boat, he met the other American captain and the Nigerian crew. One of the conditions for the companies working out of Nigeria was employing a certain percentage of their workers from the country. Nigeria's population is split almost fifty-fifty between Christian and Muslim religions. The Nigerian crewmembers were Christian. They told Rich about the lives of the people of Nigeria, their small villages, and their extreme poverty. It was a stark contrast to our lives here in the United States.

After Rich had worked overseas for almost two years, we had gotten into a routine—life with Daddy at work and life with him at home. We planned a family summer road trip for his month home. Our oldest son had just finished junior high school and would start high school in August. Our youngest was transitioning from elementary school to his first year of junior high. We took the boys and my parents to California, where my mom had spent some time as a child. We drove through west Texas and then through New Mexico, where we toured Carlsbad Caverns, hiking down the Natural Entrance Trail about 750 feet below ground. We explored the caverns and went to the amphitheater at dusk to watch the bats tornado up out of the blackness of the cavern. The next day, we drove on to White Sands National Park. The sands made out of gypsum reflected the sun as we got out of our minivan and walked through the Interdune Boardwalk and Dune of Life Nature Trail, learning about the plants and wildlife that made their home in the alien landscape. Leaving New Mexico, we drove to

Arizona and visited the Grand Canyon—Wow! What a breathtaking sight! God has made so many wonders for us to enjoy in this world. I don't think manmade buildings can compete with the beauty of nature.

We continued our journey to Yosemite National Park in California, renting a cabin inside Yosemite. We took our time exploring-trekking up mountain trails alongside rushing waterfalls that sprayed their cooling shower in the heat of the day, watching the sun off of Half Dome, barely able to make out the climbers challenging the cliff as they worked their way up its craggy face, and walking on paths that circled through ancient Giant Sequoyah trees. After three days, we headed up the California coast on the twisting, turning Pacific Coast Highway that runs along the cliffs. We hugged the mountainside, watching the crashing surf below. At Crescent City, we hiked the forests of Redwood trees that had been growing for hundreds of years. I felt like we were walking through the silence of those misty forests into a distant past, our feet crunching the pine needles that lay in beds along the forest floor. I wouldn't have been surprised to see some prehistoric creature peering behind the thick trunks of the Redwoods. I know many people long to see the cities of the world, enjoy the theater, and shop in their elegant boutiques, but I'll take the splendor of the national parks every time.

On the return journey, we came back through Salt Lake City, where Rich's dad, Brian, and his stepmom, Ellie, lived. We wanted to spend some time with them and were able to celebrate Father's Day together. After saying goodbye to them, we visited Dinosaur Park and Colorado. Rich had grown up in Winter Park, and we decided to stay a few days there. He wanted to show us the mountains he had skied in as a child. In the summer, they had turned the ski slopes into downhill mountain bike trails, and we got kitted up into protective gear and bounced on rented mountain bikes through their downhill park trail. We went on from there to Durango, Colorado, and stayed up the mountain at Purgatory. My sister and her husband had told us about Mesa Verde, so we swung by there and hiked the cliff dwellings. Then we headed home. I remember this vacation so clearly, probably because of what happened later that fall.

Once we got home, we went to the animal shelter to adopt a puppy. My beloved Lady Faith had died the previous year. I loved her so much that it was hard to even think about getting another dog. Our yellow Lab, Sis, had developed a nervous disposition since Lady's death and moved her attachment from Lady to me. Sis became very dependent on me, and after we got back from our vacation, she started panting and became

nervous when I left her home alone. We thought it would help her to have another dog in the house to play with and that she wouldn't be as lonely when I had to go back to work and the boys started back to school. We visited three or four animal shelters looking for a puppy to train until we found a little black-and-white mix. We brought her home, and the boys named her Molly. She settled in with our cats and Sis, and they became fast friends. She would curl right up next to Sis to fall asleep, and the anxiety issues our Lab had shown disappeared.

We took Rich to the airport a week later to fly out for his two-month hitch in Nigeria. I started getting the boys' school supplies and preparing what I needed to start my new high school test coordinator job. With our oldest son starting high school and our youngest leaving elementary school to begin junior high, I had to make a career decision. Even though we lived outside of the school district, our children had always attended the schools where I worked. The three levels had different starting times, and there was no way, with the distance I drove to work, that I could make all three times: myself to elementary, Ray to junior high, and Little Rich to high school. The high school Little Rich wanted to attend had an opening for a testing coordinator, a position I knew very little about. I prayed that if it were God's will for Little Rich to attend school there, He would make a way. God opened a door for me, and I was hired for the job on the understanding that when the school population grew large enough to hire a second librarian, the position would be mine.

I have often sat down to write about this next part of our lives. Anxiety rises within me as I recall the events after our summer travels. Even after going through posttraumatic stress counseling, I have continued battling panic attacks throughout the years. They begin with a feeling of dread, nausea rises in my stomach, and my heart beats erratically. I have learned to recognize the sensation for what it is, but it is still frightening. Over time, I have come to realize that we live in the world, and terrible things happen to all of us. Being a Christian doesn't mean we don't face sickness, tragedy, pain, sorrow, or death. But as Christians, God walks with us through it all. We are never alone, even during our darkest times. God holds us in His hands, which is what He did for me when my husband was kidnapped while captaining a supply vessel off the coast of Nigeria. The fourteen days that followed changed our lives forever.

Chapter 2

"Ray—you need to get up and get in the shower now! We're going to be late for school." My days started early, usually around 5:00 a.m. I got up, exercised on the elliptical for half an hour, showered, and woke Ray and our oldest son, Little Rich. This morning, though, our oldest had 6:00 a.m. basketball practice. He had spent the night in town with a friend so he could get an extra hour of sleep in the morning and still make it to practice on time. I made breakfast, got ready for work, and fed the dogs and cats while Ray showered and dressed for school.

I was so excited that morning. It was the Friday before Thanksgiving, and I was looking forward to the week of vacation. A few days earlier, my husband and I had celebrated our wedding anniversary. Well, we planned to celebrate it when he got home from this hitch on the boat. He had been within satellite phone range and called me to wish me a happy anniversary. We exchanged cards before he left and opened them on our anniversary. With Rich's schedule, our family was used to celebrating holidays and special events at various times—flexibility was vital in our lives. The boys often had two birthday celebrations and two Christmases—one when Daddy was home and one on their actual birthdays or Christmas.

It was around 6:30 a.m. when I heard the phone ring. My mind went into panic mode. I never got calls that early in the morning, so I worried that something had happened to my parents or our son at basketball practice. "I'll get it"—I called out to Ray from my bedroom. I picked up the phone. "Hello," I answered, confused, seeing the long international phone number on the caller ID. A masculine voice came over the phone, "Is this Mrs. Stephanie Tarpey?" "Yes," my stomach began knotting up. My

husband—I thought—something has happened to Rich. "Wife of Richard Tarpey?" Again, I fought the panic that rose inside of me.

I began, "Yes, I am married to Captain Richard Tarpey." He cut me off before I could say anything more. "I am from the Nigerian Embassy. I am sorry to inform you that your husband's ship was hijacked earlier this morning while returning to port. The Nigerian crewmembers were beaten and left on the boat. The American captains and the engineer from Mexico were taken hostage by a militant group." "No," my mind screamed, not realizing I had cried out loud. I sank to the floor, gasping, as Ray ran into my bedroom. "What's wrong, Momma!" He knelt beside me, wrapping his arm around my shoulder.

"I don't know yet," I cried. I heard questions distantly coming from the phone. I brokenly explained that I was hanging up now and going to call my husband's company. This must be a mistake, I thought. Rich's company contact would have called me if there was a problem, not a stranger from Nigeria. How did I know if he was even from the Embassy in Nigeria? I called Rich's satellite cell phone, but the voice answering said robotically, "The person you are trying to reach is not available at this time." Praying silently, I got up from the floor. I went to the computer, looking for Rich's company contact's phone number we had saved for emergencies. Ray followed me, his bright blue eyes dark with tears as I phoned the company. I was waiting for someone to answer, and I realized it was too early for anyone to be at the company office. I told Ray to call his aunt Darla, my sister, from his cell phone. "Ray, tell her what is happening and ask her to call Grandmamma and Granddad to let them know."

Rich had also left his supervisor's cell number, and I decided to call it since no one was in the office, but then I realized I also had the boat satellite number on my past call history. Rich had called me from the number once when he had no service. I found the call history on my cell phone and the boat number. Trembling, I pressed the number and waited for the boat phone to ring. After what seemed like hours but was only a few minutes, one of the Nigerian crew answered. I asked for Captain Rich, identifying myself as his wife Stephanie. I heard him call out to someone on the boat, and then he replied, "Captain Rich is down in the engine room. I will tell him you called."

Shaking, I hung up the phone and dialed Rich's supervisor's cell number. He answered on the first ring. Apologizing since it was so early. I told him who I was and about the phone call I had received from someone purporting

to be from the Nigerian Embassy. In my mind, I kept praying, God, please don't let this be true. Let Rich be okay, please, Lord. I heard his supervisor say, "Who did you say called?" I said again, "The Nigerian Embassy."

He responded, "I'm sorry. I don't know how they could have known so quickly before our office in Nigeria even knew anything. We just heard from the men there. Captain Richard, Captain Tim, and Antonio, the engineer, have been taken from the boat during a hijacking." I cried out, "No, it can't be true! How could this have happened? I thought they were under escort to and from the oil fields!" He answered, "We're still trying to find out what happened. I will be on a conference call with our office in Nigeria and will call you back." My thoughts circled around the morning's calls and my husband. I called the boat again, and the man who answered the phone told me to contact the company. I knelt on the floor with Ray, and we started praying, "God, please take care of Rich. Don't let them harm or hurt him in any way. Bring him back to us."

I called Rich's cell phone again to hear his voice and listen to his messages I had saved on my phone. I was still in shock, not really accepting what had happened, but knowing deep down it was true—this was not just a nightmare or a mistake. Rich's boat had been hijacked, and he had been kidnapped. I felt helpless as the fear of what the men who had taken Rich could or would do to him overwhelmed my spirit. My mind began going to dark places. I pictured Rich being threatened and beaten. Torture scenes from movies I had seen ran through my mind.

I remembered the news stories of pirate hijackings of ships off the coast of Somalia and their trademark of killing the captains and crewmembers on board. Realizing that these thoughts were not helping Rich, our children, or myself, I began repeating, "For God has not given us a spirit of fear; but of power, and of love, and of a sound mind" (2 Timothy 1:7 NKJV). As I focused on the verse, I took deep, slow breaths, calming my mind and body. I again prayed, "Please, God, let him be all right; don't let them torture or hurt him in any way. Bring him home."

Mom and Dad got to my house about thirty minutes later. I asked my parents to go to the school gym, pick up our oldest son from basketball practice, and bring him home. I called my close friend Abby, Little Rich's friend's mom, and a counselor where I worked and choked out the words explaining what had happened. I asked her to tell the principal so he would know that I would be out for a while. My sister had called her school to let them know she wouldn't be in. We had worked together at my same elementary school

for many years, and I had close, supportive friends there. I told my sister that she could let them know what was happening. They at once began praying for Rich, the two men with him, and our family.

Then came two more difficult calls, one to Rich's dad, Brian, and his wife, Ellie, in Salt Lake City, and the other to his mom, Josie, in Houston. It wasn't easy trying to explain to them their son was missing, taken by hijackers in Nigeria, and make myself understood through the tears. I didn't have answers to their questions besides what the company had told me. "God, please get us through this," I prayed. "Don't let Rich suffer or die. Please bring your mercy on him and Tim and Antonio." I waited for the phone to ring—for Rich's company or someone, anyone, to call that could give me more information about my husband.

The doorbell rang, and Ray ran to unlock the deadbolt. It was my sister, Darla, and her husband, Daniel. They began talking to Ray as they came through the door, and then I felt myself wrapped in their arms. Darla told me that Carla, my ex-principal, and Natalia, a close friend from the school where I used to work, wanted to drive out and see me to offer support. I knew Abby was coming out, too, so I told my sister they could come when she did. It honestly didn't even register with me. I focused on the phone, waiting for it to ring and trying not to think of what could happen to my husband. Time seemed to stand still as shock numbed my body and my mind. My parents and Little Rich arrived. He sat by me, and Ray sat on the other side. I held on to each of the boys' hands while my parents, my sister, and her husband discussed the situation. Their words were just background noise. I couldn't follow their conversation. I was focused on trying to keep myself together.

When the phone rang, I saw a Louisiana number and knew it must be someone from Rich's company. I didn't want to pick up the phone—fear kept my hand hovering for a moment, and then I answered the call. "Stephanie," I recognized Rich's supervisor's voice as he started to speak. Although I was listening, I felt like I was not there in the moment. It was almost as if I was out of my body, watching myself, listening and talking on the phone, and numbness settled over me again. I prayed silently while he gave me the facts, "During the hijacking, Rich, Tim, and Antonio were taken hostage. The Nigerian crewmembers were beaten and left on the boat. We haven't heard anything from the pirates yet, but we believe they won't harm them because they will want the highest possible ransom for the men. The kidnappers know they won't get that if their hostages are hurt or damaged."

He continued, "I will call you back and let you know as soon as we hear anything. We don't want to let this get out in the media because we don't know what the militant group might do if that happens."

I assured him that I would not speak to the press and would tell Rich's parents not to talk to anyone. I also asked him to give my phone number to Tim and Antonio's wives so they could call me if they heard anything. Tim's wife was from Nigeria, and they had a young daughter. She still had contact with her family there, so I hoped they might have heard rumors about the men's kidnapping and shared them with her. I looked at the clock and couldn't believe it had only been a couple of hours since I had gotten the call from the Nigerian Embassy. It felt like days. I phoned Rich's mom, his dad, and stepmom again to let them know I had spoken to the company and that we wanted to ensure that the news about the hijacking and kidnapping didn't reach the media for the men's safety. They assured me they would not talk about it with anyone but the most immediate family members.

My next thought was to ask for prayer for my husband and the other two men who were taken. I asked my father to call our church minister and tell him what was happening, that we were asking for prayer for their safe return, and that it needed to be kept off social media and out of the press. I didn't realize that prayer was already going out for the men—some of the employees from Rich's company attended church together and had requested prayer. The principal from the school I had worked at and where my sister still taught had asked for prayer from the staff, and many of them had contacted prayer chains from their churches. My mother-in-law had also requested prayer at her church in Houston.

I went into my bedroom, shut the door, and curled up into a little ball, crying out to God for His mercy and grace over the situation and for His protection over Rich, Tim, and Antonio. After another hour, my mother came to get me to let me know that Abby, Carla, and Natalia had arrived. They brought food and hugs and tried to comfort me, but I was still in a daze. As I was going over the events of the morning, I felt like I was looking at myself talking to my friends about the hijacking. It seemed like someone else's voice was relating the information while I was only listening in. Maybe the level of pain I felt was desensitizing me to everything outside my mind and thoughts. I don't know how to explain it. The only time I felt like myself was when I was alone with God. When I was praying, I could

allow myself to let go. I could reveal my genuine emotions and the terror I felt over the thought of what Rich was suffering at the hands of the pirates.

My friends left, and my sister and brother-in-law went to get dinner for all of us. My father took the boys outside to shoot baskets, and I went to lie down and wait for a phone call from someone who hopefully had more information for me. I kept imagining the phone would ring; I would answer it and hear my husband's voice on the other end of the line. I stared at the ceiling in our bedroom, visualizing scenes from our life together.

Chapter 3

We had been through so much to get to where we were as a family. I thought back to when I first met Rich. It was love at first sight. I know that is a cliché, but the minute I saw him across the room with his long, sun-bleached hair in a ponytail and deep greenish-blue eyes, I couldn't get my mind off him. I was out with my sister and some friends at the time, and when I saw him, I told her I had to meet him. It was a crazy time, and I was not in the best of places in my life. I had known Jesus Christ as my Savior since I was young, but I had not been living a Christian life. I was going along with the crowd, wanting to please my friends and be a part of the group.

Rich was very different from other men that I had dated. We rushed into our relationship, not really knowing very much about each other but feeling deep inside that we belonged together. We married quickly. From the beginning, I knew he drank daily and was an alcoholic. However, I didn't really understand much about the hold an addiction could have on you or even about the actual disease of alcoholism. I also knew he had used drugs in the past. It was not as if I hadn't been around drug use. I had friends in college who had experimented with drugs, mainly marijuana. I didn't know many who were using drugs daily, and I didn't realize that Rich was addicted to drugs as well as alcohol.

Our life together was chaotic. Rich and I continued a partying lifestyle that was common on the island where we met, and Rich lived. The island is a vacation spot, and only a few residents live there permanently. Most people working at restaurants, clubs, hotels, and businesses live off the island in one of the surrounding communities. The vacationers come to relax, soak up the sun, enjoy the beach, go fishing, and dance at the

clubs. It is also a Spring Break party destination for thousands of high school and college students.

We rented a two-story house on the bay, and my sister, Darla, lived on the first floor. We had to have a fenced backyard since Rich and I had two dogs, and Darla had a dog, too. I had Lady, a border collie who had been with me since she was three weeks old. I had wanted a puppy for a year or two, and one of the teachers I worked with had mentioned it to her daughter, who ran the nearby animal shelter. One day, Martha came to the library and told me her daughter had just called her. She wanted to let me know that they had three border collie puppies that had been brought into the shelter.

A couple of men were working at the landfill and were using equipment to move dirt over an area ready to be covered. One of the men saw a garbage bag moving around and decided to investigate. As he neared the bag, he heard whimpering and called his coworker over. He ran around mounds of garbage and dirt and ripped open the bag. Three balls of black and white fur rolled out. The men bundled them up and grabbed a box. They put the puppies into the box, and the three babies curled together in the corner. The rescuers delivered the puppies to the animal shelter. The workers named the three dogs—Faith, Hope, and Charity. The puppies were about three weeks old. The veterinarian at the animal shelter said they were border collie puppies and someone had abused them. They had taken scissors and clipped notches into their ears, which had become infected.

I took the afternoon off work and went straight to the shelter, where I met with Martha's daughter. She took me into the back room to see the puppies. I instantly fell in love with the runt, Faith. She nuzzled up to me and began sucking my finger. I named her Lady Faith because, growing up, we had always had dogs named Lady. I bottle-fed her per the veterinarian's directions, and she slept beside me on my bed. She was so sweet, but she hated it when I left her at home to go to work. Puppies love to chew, and Lady was no exception. She destroyed several telephone books. Once, I came home to find one shoe from each pair of shoes in my closet in a big circle on the floor. She dragged each one from the closet and nibbled a bit from each heel.

Lady and I formed a strong bond. We also had a chocolate Labrador retriever puppy that we named Coco Bueno. She was a roly-poly little dog, so loveable. My sister had a black Lab mix rescued from the animal shelter called Cinders. Lady and Cinders had been around each other almost daily

CHAPTER 3

while growing up, and they looked after the new addition, Coco. When I took the dogs for walks, Coco would cry because her paws got sore from the pavement. Lady and Cinders would stop walking until I picked her up and carried her. Now, I see people pushing small baby buggies for dogs. That is what I needed for Coco.

I also had two cats. Callie was our cat when I was growing up in Oklahoma. She was a beautiful yellow, white, and gray calico. Mom and Dad had retired early and moved near my sister and me. They brought Callie with them and gave her to me since I had a fenced yard, and they were moving into a townhome. The last member of our menagerie was Lucky, a black and white cat I had rescued as a kitten. She had been stuck on the atrium roof in the middle of my house. I had been allergic to cats ever since I could remember. My mom told me that when I was young, I had a kitten and a neighbor's dog attacked and killed it in front of me. After that, I had an allergic reaction whenever I was around a cat. I guess rescuing Lucky cured me of that.

All our pets were very loved members of our family. Across the street from our house by the bay was a salt marsh area, and we could see one of our friend's houses one street over. Lady and Cinders learned how to open the gate to the yard, and our friend would phone us reporting that three renegade dogs were out chasing the seabirds in the marsh. Funny, Coco's paws never seemed to hurt her when she was running through the wetland. Rich would drive home, round up the escapees, and wash all three mud-splattered dogs.

Rich was working a lot of hours as a deckhand for a charter boat, and summer was the busy season. He loved being out on the ocean and trolling for fish, even if he didn't reel them in. As educators, Darla and I were off work for the summer, so we took care of almost everything at the house. I remember one time we clogged up the sink with potato peelings, and we didn't know how we were going to clear it without calling a plumber. A friend of ours brought over an electric drill that he attached to a plumber's snake. He gave us directions, "Put the snake down the sink, and one of you stand over there to operate the drill." I started feeding the snake into the drain. Darla was on the other side of the room, standing on the couch to get leverage. She turned on the drill—the snake started whipping around, and so did we, almost turning flips—screaming, while slimy potato peelings flew up out of the sink like a geyser—what a mess! We collapsed onto the floor, laughing until we cried. It took the three of

us a couple of hours to clean up the potato peelings that were stuck to the floor and the walls. We even found some on the ceiling. We had a lot of fun times living in that house on the bay.

At the end of the fishing season, Rich and I had a long talk about his future work plans. We knew that even with my income as a librarian, he needed a higher-paying job than he made working as a deckhand, which only lasted for three or four months a year during the fishing season. He had logged enough hours working on boats to become a licensed captain if he passed the required classes and tests. We started all the paperwork and looked at the cost of him attending the classes and testing. He also talked to another friend of his who was interested in getting his license, too.

In December, Rich and his friend went together to the maritime school in Houston so they could share the expense of a hotel room for the three weeks the class met. They both passed. Rich's friend got his six-pack license for charter fishing, and Rich got his 500-ton license so he could run crew boats in the offshore oil industry. After they returned, Rich worked off and on as a deckhand for a fishing charter boat and helped a friend in his landscaping business. He also began looking at offshore oil companies to see who was hiring. We discussed the type of schedule he would have to follow, which usually involved being gone for three weeks and home for ten days or one month on the boat and two weeks at home.

Our marriage was definitely not easy. We had both been married before, and we knew it would take work to stay together. I became pregnant with our first child, and we decided that Rich would wait to apply for a crew boat captain position until after our baby was born. We started looking for a new place to move to because the rent was too expensive at the house on the bay for the three of us. Darla moved into a duplex down the street from where we were living. We had more difficulty finding an affordable place to live with a fenced backyard.

My mom and sister went house hunting with me, and we finally found a townhome that allowed pets, had a fenced backyard, and had two bedrooms so we could have a nursery for our baby. Darla and I re-purposed some old furniture, painting it white and stamping aqua, lime green, and navy ocean creatures on the shelves and dresser for the baby's room. I dreaded growing huge and being around all the spring break girls in their bikinis, so I tried to keep in shape, walking and exercising on my elliptical and taking the dogs on a daily trek while I was pregnant. We lived five minutes from my sister and twenty minutes from my parents.

CHAPTER 3

We had great neighbors, and the small, fenced backyard was perfect for our dogs. There was a deck on the roof where we watched the island's weekly fireworks with our family.

My legs began swelling during the last month of my pregnancy. I developed pre-eclampsia and had to go on bed rest. My doctor was very attentive and ran tests on me each day. She decided to induce my labor about two weeks early because she was worried that I would go into eclampsia, endangering my baby and risking my life if I carried him to full term. The delivery was difficult, and our son had to go into the neonatal unit with jaundice when he was born. He was there for three days, and we were so excited when we finally got to bring him home. Although we had set up a nursery in one of the bedrooms, I wanted his crib next to our bed so I could check on him through the night. We named him after my husband and my father—Richard Ray Tarpey—we called him Little Rich. He was such a good baby. Little Rich was beautiful and looked so much like my husband.

Soon after he was born, my husband's aunt sent him photos of his mom and his biological father. Rich looked exactly like him. I couldn't believe how closely they resembled each other. His biological father and Rich's mother had been young when they married. We did some research online and found his phone number. One night, Rich called him to reach out since he had never known him. No one had told him anything about the man who had fathered him. When Rich phoned, he and his father talked for a long time. My husband found out that his father had joined the military soon after Rich's birth. He and Rich's mom split up, and he had allowed Brian, Josie's new husband, the father who had raised Rich, to adopt him and his younger brother, Jeff. Rich's biological father had remarried and had two daughters. Rich told him a little about himself and that we had a son. It was good for Rich to find out about his birth father. He had always believed that the man who raised him, Brian, was his biological father until he found his birth certificate listing another name as his father. He had a lot of trust issues stemming from the fact that he hadn't known he was adopted, and finding out the truth about his parentage helped him deal with those.

Since our son was born at the end of April, I was able to stay home with him on maternity leave from his birth through August, when school started back. It was such a blessing as a working mother to be able to stay home with him those first three months. I loved being a mother, and celebrating my first Mother's Day as a mom still stands out in my mind.

While my husband worked deckhanding for a charter fishing boat during those summer months, I enjoyed my time at home with our baby. I read to him and laid him on my chest and stomach to nap. I took him to the baby pool at my parent's condo, and he enjoyed the warmth of the water and kicking his feet to see the splashes. He loved our dogs and cats, although the felines gave his groping hands a wide berth. We all doted on him and took him with us everywhere.

August came too soon, and it was back to work for me. My parents had volunteered to take care of our baby during the day if I would bring him to their house. What a gift and a relief! With my parents, I knew he would get the best care from people who loved him dearly. I had to get up early to drop off Little Rich at their home. My husband would hold our baby boy and give him a bottle while I showered and got ready for work. Sometimes, I would walk back into the bedroom and find our son asleep on my drowsing husband's chest while cartoons played on the television. I left a lot of baby supplies at my parent's condo, but I still packed a diaper bag each day. I fastened Little Rich into his baby car seat and picked up my sister, and we drove to our parents to drop him off and then to the school where my sister and I both worked. I was the school librarian, and she was a fourth-grade teacher there. I loved my job. Working with children and sharing my lifelong love of reading was a joy. I also loved being a mother. I was a Christian and went to church, but I was still not putting God first in my life. I was busy with family, work, and enjoying the island's lifestyle. I was thankful for all God had given me, but my mind and heart were not focused on Him.

As the fishing season drew to a close and I went back to work, we realized Rich needed to find a job that would help with all our bills, especially now that we had a baby and the hospital bills from his birth and his stay in the neonatal unit were huge, even with my health insurance. Rich began applying for jobs captaining in the oil and gas industry, and he was hired by a large offshore oil company to captain a crew boat running supplies and workers to the rigs. He worked for that company only a short time. As an alcoholic, Rich couldn't handle the fact that you were on a boat for two weeks and couldn't drink. He quit that company and was soon hired by another. That one worked out longer. Rich worked there for the fall and winter seasons but missed home, so he quit and returned to the island to run a parasail boat during spring and summer break. It was not the best environment for him, and he was soon drinking daily. He took a second job as a deckhand on a private fishing boat for tournaments to help make ends meet.

CHAPTER 3

I had a very traditional upbringing. My parents had grown up going to church, and I was raised attending church. I also grew up in a small community and was very sheltered, so I did not recognize the signs that my husband was going down a dark road. I knew he was drinking too much, and I drank with him, not to the degree he did, but enough to block the symptoms of the more significant problem in our lives. I became pregnant with our second child when our first son was about two and a half years old. I thought that was ideal because my sister and I were three years apart, and we were very close. Rich and I found a larger house to rent in a community near the island since our family was expanding.

Rich's stepfather, Ken, whom he was very close to, died during the first few months of my pregnancy. Ken had been Rich's lifeline when he was younger and had given him a home when Rich had nowhere to go. Ken's death really sent Rich into a tailspin. He didn't know how to handle the sadness and anger he felt from losing someone so close, and I tried to help him, but I couldn't be with him 24/7. We had a hurricane coming up from the Atlantic, and Rich was unable to leave to go to Ken's funeral in Michigan. Guilt from being unable to be there compounded the emotions he was already feeling from losing a mentor and father figure in his life.

Alcohol was not enough to numb the pain Rich was experiencing, so he turned to cocaine and other drugs to block his emotions. I knew his use of alcohol had increased to drinking all day, but I didn't realize he had progressed to using drugs. Rich started losing a lot of weight and staying away from home, making excuses that he had to work or needed to help a friend. He wouldn't admit anything to me, but his words were often garbled when we talked. Money started disappearing from our bank account. Even now, thinking about this, I remember the sick feeling in my stomach as I began to see the problem for what it was. I started missing spoons from the kitchen, not forks or knives, just spoons. I had no idea what that meant. Later, a drug rehab counselor told me Rich was using them when he prepared cocaine to snort.

I feel so stupid about not seeing what was right in front of me. I was busy with work, our son, and my pregnancy, so I didn't realize what was happening until Rich started staying out all night. He made excuses—that he got off work from the boat, ate at this friend's house, and fell asleep, or that the causeway had shut down from an accident and he couldn't get across. Of course, I called his cell phone nonstop when he didn't come home, and when he didn't answer, I sat in a panic, trying to calm myself down. I was

seven months pregnant, waking our three-year-old son up in the middle of the night, carrying him in his pajamas to the car, and strapping him into his car seat so I could go look for my husband in the small towns surrounding us on the highway and through neighborhoods.

I was angry with him and afraid that he might be hurt. I will never forget driving down those dark roads searching for his car and the desperation and terror in my mind, thinking I would find him on the side of the road or unconscious somewhere. I even called the police station and hospitals looking for him. I confronted Rich, but he always made excuses and never admitted what was going on. I prayed and prayed for him and over our lives. God carried me in His arms through all of this. He loved me, held me, and brought me through the pain and shadows then, just as He will today.

Then, one day, sitting at church with my parents, my father gasped and slumped in his chair. I was eight months pregnant, and I was sitting next to him. I touched his shoulder and said, "Dad, are you alright?" When he didn't answer me, I interrupted our minister's sermon, calling out, "Help—somebody please help!" The woman behind daddy was a nurse in a cardiac unit—thank you, Lord! She felt for his pulse and then picked him up from his slump with both arms across his chest, like a hug from the back. He regained consciousness and began breathing. She later explained they used this hold with cardiac patients to restart their hearts.

In the meantime, one of the church members phoned for an ambulance. When the ambulance arrived, the nurse told us to make sure they tested him with the twenty-four-hour cardiac enzyme test. She insisted that we make sure they admitted him overnight so they could run all three of the tests because when she had checked his pulse, she had not been able to find one. At the hospital, they thought it was just indigestion and wanted to release him. His echocardiogram, electrocardiogram, and cardiac enzyme test had all come back in the normal ranges. Still, because of what the nurse had told us, Mom insisted they keep him and run the entire gamut of tests. On the third marker, taken the following day, the enzyme test showed that Dad had experienced a heart attack. We had him transported by ambulance to a heart hospital in a larger city about an hour away because it had an excellent success rate.

After more testing, the doctors found that he needed a quadruple bypass. I remember the long hours of sitting at the hospital that day, continuously praying that the surgery would be successful. I also prayed that I would not go into labor right in the middle of Dad's surgery. We were

so thankful when the surgeon came to the waiting room and told us that the bypass surgery was a success and that our father had come through it very well. My sister and I went to the hospital daily during our father's recovery. Mom stayed with Dad for as long as they would allow. I sat in the lobby with our three-year-old son each day, waiting for my turn to go in to see him. I was loaded down with a bag full of Little Rich's toys, activities, and snacks to keep him occupied. My husband was working, but I did not trust him to stay sober and care for our son even when he was off. Daddy's recovery at the hospital went smoothly. We took him home with a stuffed heart pillow and lots of love and relief when he was released. Our son still has that pillow. We gave thanks to God for Dad's life and for bringing him through safely.

About a week after we brought our father home, I started getting contractions. Since I had pre-eclampsia during my first pregnancy, I was watching out for the symptoms I had experienced —blood rushing to my head and swelling of my legs. I had a different obstetrician with my second pregnancy. When I began having those symptoms again, I spoke to him about the pre-eclampsia, the swelling I was experiencing, and the tingling in my head. He reassured me that everything was going well with the baby and me. I questioned him, but I went along with his diagnosis because I was distracted by my father's surgery and worried about my husband's erratic behavior.

When I went into labor, we found out that my body was having issues. I had a wonderful nurse in the hospital. She stayed past her shift so she could remain with me throughout the delivery. She was worried about me because my blood pressure was erratic. I was chilling and trembling so severely that they couldn't warm me up. They covered me in blankets, but I couldn't stop shaking. The doctor came in, and delivery started. The labor was difficult, and I heard the doctor tell them to get surgery ready in case he had to do an emergency C-section. My mom and husband were praying with me in the labor room. The doctor used forceps to help bring my son into the world, and he had to go into the neonatal ICU for a few days. I was thankful God got me through that delivery with a beautiful, healthy baby. We named him Ray Curtis Tarpey, after my father and a man who was like a father to Rich. After a few days, we brought Ray home, and I thought things with my husband would improve. I was in denial, thinking that now that my father was getting better and we had our new baby, Rich could straighten himself up and get his life back. How naive I was.

Rich didn't get any better. He made lots of promises, but the lies continued, and he spiraled deeper into alcohol and drug use. One time, I saw a text on his phone, and what it said chilled me to the bone. His dealer—who I thought was some guy who came down from the upper Valley and went fishing with him—texted that it would be a shame for something to happen to his house or wife or children if he didn't pay what he owed. I confronted Rich, and he broke down, confessing that he hadn't been able to quit using. He had not been going to the AA meetings that he had promised to attend. Instead, he had been going to a friend's house to drink and get high. I told him that we couldn't keep going on in this way. I couldn't live life like this anymore, and I wouldn't let my children grow up in a home with a father who was slowly killing himself with drugs and alcohol. He agreed to go into a drug rehab center, and we found one that took our medical insurance in the Hill Country of Texas. That was really important because Rich's drug use also affected us financially. We were basically living on our credit cards at this point since he had cleaned our account out to pay off his dealer.

My parents took care of the boys, and my sister took care of the pets so I could drive Rich up to rehab. God is the only reason we got through that trip. The six-hour drive to the hill country was a nightmare. Rich wanted to contact his dealer to get one more hit before we left home. He thought he would be able to have someone meet him at a gas station to drop off a package on the way up and he kept insisting that we stop so he could go to the bathroom or get something to drink. I didn't want to stop for anything because I was afraid Rich would take off. Finally, I gave in, and we pulled into a station, but I never left him alone, so he never had a chance to make any calls to arrange a pick-up or drop-off. Rich was experiencing withdrawals. He was shaky and nauseous, taking his anger out on me since I was the only one around. He finally fell asleep for a couple of hours, and we drove into the rehab parking lot late that night. It was dark, so I couldn't see any of the area or the facilities.

My heart was broken, but I knew this was my husband's only chance. Rich fought going in, wanting to wait another day, but I left him with the personnel there and prayed he would be okay. I went to stay at a hotel in a nearby town. I didn't think I would be able to sleep because I was so keyed up, and I felt like my heart was breaking, but I passed out as soon as my head hit the pillow. I returned to the rehab center the next day to verify the paperwork and insurance, but I didn't see Rich or speak to him. The doctor told me he was going through withdrawals from cocaine and also

from alcohol. They had him on medication, and he was sleeping. I gave them all of my contact information and headed home. The tears streamed down my face as I drove away.

The pain of leaving him hit as soon as the numbness from getting through the last six or seven months and trying to hold our family and home together wore off. Here I was with a three-year-old, a three-month-old, and a husband who was battling addiction. We were getting even deeper into debt now from rehab bills, and I was in so much pain. Looking back now, I can see that during the whole ordeal, God was carrying me. He lifted me in his arms in my despair and kept me sane. Rich called me every three or four days from a pay phone at the rehabilitation center.

The first week was tough for him as he went through severe physical, mental, and emotional withdrawals, but they had the medical team to help him through it. Rich was doing well—working through things from his early life with the counselors and going through the recovery process. He met other people fighting the same addictions and was able to talk to them about issues he had been having for years. He was getting the support and help he needed to realize what life had become for him. They took him back to his childhood to see how his addictions had started at an early age.

My life was filled with work and taking care of two small children. My family and my boss were a great support during this time. I held it together at work and in front of people, focusing on anything but what was happening in my home life. There were times, though, that no matter how hard I tried not to think about it, the pain just rose within me, and the tears rolled down my cheeks. I remember shopping at HEB, pushing my cart down the aisle, and just starting to cry, unable to stop the tears running down my face. I left my cart, full of groceries, in front of the bread aisle and walked out. I was mourning the loss of my husband, our dreams of a life together, and the family we had become.

Rich's counselor called me after the third week of his treatment. He told me they had a weekly family meeting with co-counseling and wanted to see if I could come up for it. Rich's release at the end of the month of rehab would depend on his progress and what they saw support-wise from the home he would be returning to. I took a week's leave from work. My parents agreed to take care of our boys. My sister helped by feeding and caring for our pets. God really blessed me with a wonderfully supportive family. They were always there to help us and care for the boys and our pets, enabling me to help Rich and myself. I booked a room at a bed and breakfast close to the

rehab center and drove up to the Hill Country. I didn't know what to expect, but I was ready to participate and see what would happen.

Since I had driven up in the dark before, I hadn't been able to see all the beauty of the area. The land was striking, surrounded by hills with rivers winding throughout. It was autumn, and the leaves of the trees were turning yellow, orange, and red. The hillsides were beautiful, patchwork quilts of color. It reminded me of the area where I grew up. I began to relax as I drove, praying that Rich had been able to work out his issues and that he would be able to come home.

The Victorian-style bed and breakfast I had booked was set back in the hills among tall oak and sycamore trees. The air was crisp and clean, and I breathed in the smell of autumn. We didn't have four seasons down at the tip of South Texas. Fall came and went there with temperatures in the nineties, and palm trees didn't have leaves that flamed into hues of fire before falling from the tree for winter. That was one thing I had really missed when I moved from Oklahoma. Fall was always one of my favorite times of the year. I checked in for my reservation. They had many guests in my situation—there to see a husband, wife, son, daughter, or loved one under treatment for drug or alcohol addiction at the nearby hill country rehab center.

My room had a queen size antique bed, a wooden floor, and braided throw rugs. The mattress felt as if it was filled with feathers. The furniture in the front lounge area was antique dark wood upholstered in deep eggplant-purple velvet. There were board games, cards, and books available on floor-to-ceiling shelves for their guests' use. The sun shone through mullioned windows, and I decided to explore the countryside before my first session with Rich's counselor. I went for a long walk behind the inn that meandered down to a river. Squirrels climbed up and down the trees, and I caught a glimpse of a shy doe on the other side of the river before she ran into the woods. What a peaceful and serene place. It was just what I needed for the week ahead.

Going through the counseling sessions, I felt positive and uplifted. I learned more about my part in the recovery process and what a person with an addiction goes through. With the help of group counseling, I realized that although Rich loved me, he could not control his addiction. Nothing I said or did could stop his craving and his use of alcohol and drugs to cope with life. I had always felt that it was on me to make him quit—that if I said or did the right thing and found the correct words, he would stop. No person has that power or control over someone else.

CHAPTER 3

Rich got to leave with me a couple of times, and we drove a short way to Stonehenge II, a replica of Stonehenge with pillars of rough, rectangular stone arranged in a circle standing in an empty field. We talked, and I felt like this was the first time he was honest with me about his condition. We went hiking up to the hilltop, where the rehab center had a retreat for their patients. They usually had their sunrise meetings there. I learned about the twelve-step program they followed. Rich had begun working through the steps to recovery, and my being there was part of that. Rich shared his process with me, and we were full of hope for our future.

I left the rehab center with the plan that Rich would come home in another week if his counselors still believed he could handle living in the environment where we lived. Rich and I had talked a lot about what was happening and everything he had been hiding from me. We opened up to each other about our beliefs and feelings and what triggered his drinking and drug usage. Although I was ready to try to work through everything at home with him, I wasn't prepared to give him access to our bank funds. I took his name off of the accounts, and we discussed the reasons I wasn't ready for him to have a way to get money out of the checking account without my knowledge. He agreed, although he wasn't happy about it, but on this point, I stayed firm. We were already in enough debt financially.

The drive to pick up Rich at the end of his four weeks at the rehab to bring him home was very different than the drive up the month before. The doctors treating him had made Rich an appointment with a psychiatrist up the Valley, who would be his contact doctor at home. Life looked promising as we drove back to our house. It was a blessing that the boys were too young to know what was happening. Little Rich was just three, and Ray was a baby. My parents and sister were incredibly supportive of me, but I know they were torn about whether I should stay with Rich. Honestly, I was conflicted also, but I prayed and prayed about it, and I didn't believe that God was leading me to leave Rich.

We got home, and my husband was so happy to see the boys and our dogs, Coco and Lady. Having him in the house was wonderful, and he went to see the psychiatrist the next day. Although he had left the treatment center totally drug-free, with no prescriptions, the doctor in McAllen placed him on medication and diagnosed him with other psychological problems. I never met the psychiatrist because he said he was only treating Rich, not me. After his appointments, Rich came home upset and depressed. He didn't agree with the psychiatrist's diagnosis, and

neither did I. The medications were affecting him, and it didn't take long to see what was happening. Rich had started sliding into his old habits. I wasn't as naive this time—I had been through this with him before.

Rich began hallucinating from one of the medications prescribed by the psychiatrist and started drinking again. He also contacted his old friends he used to party with and joined them in using drugs while I was at work. His speech became confused as if he couldn't get the words out. I remember the night of the Presidential election. The memory runs through my mind vividly, almost like a movie reel. The dark, humid night surrounded us with a few stars shining in the sky. I sat with Rich out on the front lawn—he was huddled on the grass, and I put my arms around him, praying and telling him he had to choose life—he had to choose to live, not to die because using drugs and alcohol was going to kill him. I was desperate, crying out to God to save Rich from his addictions. The Holy Spirit lifted me up; otherwise, I could not have made it through the pain and despair erupting inside me.

Two days later, I called a couple of Rich's close friends, asking for help. He hadn't come home, and I didn't know what to do. One of them told me that maybe he needed some tough love and that jail time might help him sober up, that sometimes you have to let go and let him face what he had made of his life. I couldn't let that happen if I could possibly help it. I didn't want my children to have to visit their dad in jail. Another friend, John, told me to pick him up so we could drive around some places on the island and look for Rich's car. We went to about five houses and finally found Rich's car parked near an old trailer where one of his buddies was staying.

John went in to get him while I waited outside. As John helped Rich walk to the car, I could see my husband was in bad shape. He was trembling and sweating, mumbling incoherently. We tried to find out what he had taken, but he was too out of it to tell us. I called a friend of ours, a nurse. She worked for a doctor in a nearby town and told me to take Rich to the hospital there. The doctor she assisted specialized in drug and alcohol addiction. She met us at the hospital, where they pumped his stomach and gave him fluids for dehydration. The doctor sent me home after Rich was admitted and told me to return the next day because they needed to monitor him and run more tests. I wouldn't be able to see him until the following afternoon.

I thanked John for helping me find Rich and being there for us at the emergency room. I drove him to his house, picked up our sons from my parents, and drove home. I was mentally and physically exhausted. It seemed to me like there was a fight over Rich's life—his spirit—his soul,

CHAPTER 3

and all I could do was pray, so that is what I did. Prayer is a powerful tool. Sometimes, it is the only thing we can do in a situation. God listens to His children; even in our darkest hours, He is with us.

The next day was our four-year anniversary. I drove to the hospital thinking about our time together as husband and wife and wondering if we would be able to stay together. I felt emotionally exhausted from the roller coaster we were on. Still, I was so grateful to God that Rich hadn't died. I picked up a pizza, and we ate our anniversary dinner there in his hospital room. He was tired but sober, and it wasn't easy to get through to him. I didn't really know what to do. I had hit the wall, knowing that there was absolutely nothing that I could say, no action I could take, that would change the circumstances or keep Rich sober. If Rich made it out of his addictions, it would be because of God. Rich had to be the one to make that decision—to stop fighting against it and to give God complete control over his life and his choices. I had learned that at the addiction treatment center in the Hill Country, but now I saw that Rich could not stay sober for even a couple days out of the cocoon of safety and support that rehab provided.

You always hear "to let go and let God." You don't realize the difficulty of doing that until you are faced with a situation where that is your only answer. Giving the burden of Rich's addictions to God was very freeing. It can be a heavy load to bear when you believe that you are responsible for someone's sobriety—for that person's desire to live. You believe that the words you speak will determine that person's ability to survive. I gave everything to God and prayed for His will in the situation. I turned over all my desires and control and prayed for acceptance of His path in our lives. No matter what, I knew that God was in control, and I was not. Whatever He had for us was what was best for our lives.

We met with Rich's doctor at the hospital, and he set up a stay at a rehabilitation center—a halfway house in California. It was a place he had sent his patients for drug and alcohol addiction in the past. They didn't use any chemically dependent prescription medications to treat the patient. The treatment center was more of a long-term situation than where Rich had been, transitioning from rehab to a structured halfway house with counseling and restrictions. I made the plane reservation and went home and packed Rich some clothes. When he was released from the hospital, I picked him up, took him to the airport, and said goodbye. Rich didn't come home, and he didn't see our sons before he flew out. I didn't make any promises this time. I didn't say I would be waiting for him to come home or that I would

miss him. I just prayed with him and told him I would keep praying for his recovery and that God would direct our lives. Rich was unhappy about the situation but knew this was his only hope.

I drove home alone from the airport, but I didn't cry. I was determined to go on with life. I had two children to take care of, and I needed to get back to being myself—the person I was before my focus had zoomed in on Rich's addiction. I had lived in this nightmare of loss and betrayal for so long now that I didn't recognize myself anymore. You really can lose yourself when you are in a relationship with an addict. God kept me strong through all of this. I wept, and even though things looked hopeless, the Holy Spirit was in me, keeping the hope of reaching the end of this tunnel alive in my heart. I cried out to Jesus daily. I prayed throughout the day and night, just talking to God in my mind as I went through my daily routine and work. I had two little boys who needed their mother, and I turned my time and energy toward them. I began volunteering in the church nursery, and, of course, work took up my time.

We made it through the holidays, and Rich called me almost every day. He went to sunrise recovery meetings on the beach and met with his counselor daily. Rich also started attending church in Newport Beach, giving his life to God's purpose. He transitioned pretty quickly from the rehabilitation section to the extended halfway house living situation, and this type of arrangement kept him away from the influence of his partying friends and the lifestyle he had grown up in. His only responsibility was to stay sober.

Rich mentioned over and over that he wanted us to stay together as a family. I told him that he would have to prove himself to me. I couldn't make him any promises. I didn't want our children in the situation we had been in, and I didn't want to be in that life anymore, either. You can't live in that type of stress nonstop—never knowing if the person you love and are married to is going to come home—or be in a broken down trailer somewhere overdosing on drugs, not knowing if money is going to go missing, or some drug dealer is threatening you or your children. I had to go on and make a life for them, even if it didn't work out for us to have a life together.

Rich got a part-time job moving furniture with one of the other guys in the halfway house. Seeing he could have a life and friends in sobriety was very healthy for him. He realized there were so many things in the world, and experiencing them without chemical enhancement was even better than being drunk or stoned, unable to remember what had

happened or whom he had been with. Rich eventually got a job working on a boat and moved into an apartment with a sober friend. As he started using his captain's license and working more, he began staying at a low-cost hotel when he was off the boat to avoid spending so much money on rent. Rich still attended counseling and recovery meetings when not offshore and kept in touch with his sponsor. We made it a priority to stay in touch daily when he wasn't out on the boat working.

As summer drew near, Rich began talking about me bringing the boys out to California when I was on summer break so he could see us. I told him, "Only if you save enough money from your job to pay for our flights, a hotel, and meals. In other words, the trip will have to be covered totally financially by you. You need to show me that you can stay sober and save enough money to bring us out there." He agreed and began working toward getting us together as a family again. Shortly after our youngest son turned one in July, Rich bought our plane tickets. He reserved a hotel room near the rehab center in Newport Beach, California. I was excited but also wary and nervous. I wanted everything to work out so we could be together, but more than that, I wanted God's will for our lives and the lives of our sons.

A few days before the flight, I began packing for a four-year-old, a one-year-old, and myself. Two car seats, a stroller, diapers, baby clothes, medications, clothing, baby food, and about a hundred items later, I realized the monumental task I had taken on. I had to change planes twice and tote a diaper bag with necessities, a car seat to use on the plane, and a stroller to help get through the airports. I wondered what in the world I was doing. I had never flown by myself for that distance, much less with a baby and an energetic toddler. Changing flights in Dallas was a nightmare. We were going from a small plane, which landed at a different terminal, to a jumbo jet. I had to load the boys and everything else on a bus because there wasn't a tram to take us across the landing zone to the other terminal. God really does give us the strength we need at the time we need it.

When we landed at the airport in Los Angeles, Rich was waiting to meet us. He had put on a little weight and looked healthier than he had for over a year. The airport was packed, and we got our luggage and headed to a hotel in Newport Beach. The boys and I were exhausted, so we just ordered pizza delivered to our hotel, ate, and went to sleep. The next day, we decided to go sightseeing around Newport Beach, and we went to the pier and walked around, just talking and trying to get to know each other again. Being together again as a family felt strange, but it also felt good. When the

boys napped, we spent time reviewing what had happened in the last year and what had changed that might enable us to stay together. We even talked about me getting a job in California as a librarian or teacher and relocating. We decided to drive to San Diego and take the boys to the zoo the following day. The boys had a wonderful time. Our four-year-old couldn't get enough of the "Sandinego" Zoo, as he called it. We strolled slowly so they could enjoy viewing animals they had never seen in person before. They loved the pandas and the koala bears, but the swimming polar bear was their favorite.

Just spending time together and praying together, I began adjusting to the idea that we could be a family again. Somewhere inside, though, I was ready for the other shoe to drop—for something to happen that would ultimately destroy whatever we had left. I had turned everything over to God and knew that if we stayed together, it would be by His will, not Rich's or mine. The statistics aren't great for recovering people with a substance use disorder, and only by Rich's trust and reliance on God and turning everything over to Him would he be able to stay sober. Although I didn't trust Rich in his own ability to remain clean—I did trust God to keep him on the path. Trust issues with a recovering alcoholic or addicted spouse don't just go away.

It's hard to explain that although I wanted Rich to stay sober and for us to be a family again, I also felt uneasy about it and doubtful. I had so many issues to work through, and I gave those to God for His will for our children and us. The relief that came over me as I stopped taking responsibility for us staying together and blaming myself for not preventing Rich's relapse or possible future relapses gave me a totally different outlook on our future together. When I left, we decided that Rich would keep working in California, running an offshore oil supply boat, and start flying home when he was on his two weeks off instead of staying in a hotel. It was a big step for us. I told him I would also look at my retirement system in Texas, transferring to California, and what it would take to get certified as a school librarian in California.

Before we knew it, our time was up, and Rich was due to return to the boat for work. As I boarded the plane, he and I hugged, and he held the boys tightly. I felt more hopeful for our marriage than I had in a long time. On my flight home, I met a very kind lady. I felt sorry for whoever was seated next to the boys and me, and I told her—"I am so sorry you are stuck next to us. The boys are a little tired and cranky today. I hope they won't drive you too crazy." She told me not to worry that she had

grandchildren and asked me where I was flying. I didn't go into any personal details but just said that I had taken the boys to visit my husband, that he worked in California, by the Newport Beach area, and that we were traveling back to Texas. She explained that she was a school district superintendent in northern California. "Isn't that a coincidence," I said, "I'm a school librarian." She looked at me in surprise and then offered me a job. California had just passed a ruling that they had to have certified librarians in all their schools. They had a shortage of people who met the certification requirements, and she asked me to come to work for her district. We talked the rest of the way, and the boys actually went to sleep, so the flight wasn't as stressful as I expected. She gave me her contact information, and I promised to look into the possibility of relocating.

However, moving to California didn't seem realistic by the time I got home. I would be there with Rich, but his schedule had him working offshore for a month at a time and then home for two weeks. I would not know anyone to help with the boys while I was working. In Texas, I had a very supportive administrator and faculty, and leaving my parents and sister didn't seem like a good idea. Financially, it wasn't a wise step either. We would have more expenses, like daycare, and the cost of living was higher in California. I don't know, though. Looking back, it was such a coincidence that I can't help but wonder if I missed an opportunity or door that God had opened.

Things settled back into a routine when I got home, and it wasn't long before it was time to start the new school year. My principal had been given a new school, still in the building stages, and he had taken me along as the librarian. We were located in portable buildings at three campuses while ours was under construction. I rotated between all three schools, visiting the students' classrooms with a mobile bookshelf so they could check out books. I read picture books to the Pre-K through 2nd grade students, wore a wizard's hat and gown, and read *Harry Potter and the Sorcerer's Stone* to the 3rd through 5th grade students. They loved it! When the movie came out, I took all of our 5th-grade students on a field trip to watch it. That was so fun. It was a hectic time in my career, but exactly what I needed to take my mind off my personal life.

The lease was up on the house we were renting, so I found one on the island close to the beach with a fenced backyard to rent. It was perfect for the boys and our dogs. Each day, I dropped our one-year-old at my parents by about 7:00 a.m. and then took our four-year-old with me into Brownsville to

a Christian day school for the mornings. My dad picked him up at noon each day. My parents and my sister and brother-in-law were such a tremendous help. I don't know what I would have done without them. I knew the boys were getting the best care possible while I worked.

God filled my life with a great, supportive family and caring friends to help me through the day, and I prayed during the day and night for His grace and for Rich's recovery. If I took my eyes off Jesus, I became overwhelmed and felt doubt creeping into my mind and heart. Focusing on God gave me hope and the strength to continue. Rich was working and sending money home to help with expenses. As we had planned, my husband started flying home on his two weeks off so we could work on our goal of becoming a family again. Through the grace of God, he was able to stay sober.

On September 11, 2001, I was driving into work listening to music on the radio when an announcement broke into the Christian song that was playing. Tears began running down my face as I listened to the live broadcast of a tragedy that changed how those of us living in the United States looked at the invulnerability of our country. I was in shock—a feeling I shared with millions of Americans as terrorists attacked our country, killing innocent people on their way to work. The hijacking of the airplanes, the subsequent destruction of the Twin Towers, and the attack on the Pentagon made us realize that our country was not indestructible. Brave, courageous people lost their lives that day, and we watched it live on the news and the internet as it was happening. Our country went into lockdown, and we went into mourning. Rich was due to fly home the day after the terrorist attacks, but all airline flights were canceled for the foreseeable future, so he stayed in California and volunteered to work another hitch.

Four days later, on the night of September 15, 2001, the island causeway collapsed, sending six cars barreling into the water and killing eight people. My brother-in-law, Daniel, called me to tell me, and he brought water because people were already buying up all the cases of bottled water on the island. Rumors were rampant, and it was even suggested that this was also a terrorist attack. Later, we found out that a barge had struck one of the causeway supports and caused the destruction. The causeway was the only bridge to get on and off the island. We were stranded with no way to get off except for boat transportation. Life changed drastically for all of us living there. Even though we were not in immediate physical danger, the tragic events from four days earlier, plus the collapse of our only way to the

mainland and the deaths of locals traveling home over the causeway that night, rocked our small community and families.

While America was picking up the pieces and mourning the loss of thousands of people, we were trying to figure out how to get to work without a way off of the island and get food and water. Luckily, my brother-in-law had a boat, a small Shamrock, and could ferry us across the bay to get groceries. Dad said he could pick up Darla and me and drive us to work after Daniel brought us across, so that became our short-term plan. Then, larger boats started making daily runs, ferrying residents to the mainland. We caught the boats at 5:30 in the morning, and our father picked us up, then drove to Brownsville and dropped Darla and me off at work and Little Rich at school. He and Mom then took Ray home for the day, and he drove back eight hours later to pick us all up and meet the boat at the dock so we could return home. What amazing parents God gave me!

After about three weeks, car ferries were brought down, and we were able to drive our car onto the ferry and off at the dock. We got in line for the car ferry at about 5:00 each morning. Then we dropped off Ray with my parents and drove Little Rich to his Pre-K school and on to work. It was a demanding schedule, but we made it work, and the island was so calm without any tourists. Very few cars were on the road, and the weather was beautiful. Even crossing on the ferries was a peaceful experience. When you can't rush around and are forced to slow your pace, you see and experience things around you differently. I especially remember one evening riding across on one of the shuttle boats, holding Ray in my lap with Little Rich seated next to me—the harvest moon was enormous and a brilliant orange-red color that reflected over the ocean. Surrounded by the stillness of the water, I could see so clearly the beauty God had created and His grace over our lives.

On the weekends, we walked on the beach and let the waves lap over our toes—the boys loved the boat rides and the extended beach times. My husband didn't get to come home during this time; airline flights were still on high alert, and we decided it would also be complicated to get to the airport to pick him up and take him back on time with the causeway still down. Looking back, I don't see the stress or fear during the time of the causeway collapse as much as I do the slower pace of life and time with my children. My mind has snapshot photos of the beauty that surrounded me—beauty I had taken for granted and rushed through, now slowed to a panoramic view

of waves, sand, moonlight, and the feel of small hands holding onto me as my children sat next to me on the ferry benches and on my lap.

Two months later, the causeway was set to reopen. My husband was able to get a flight into the Corpus Christi airport. I drove the three hours to pick him up. As we crossed over the newly repaired causeway, I felt a moment of fear clenching my stomach when we passed over the area that had fallen into the bay. Rich had not been home at all during the time of the closure, so he had a lot of questions, and we talked the whole way home about how life had changed for us, our community, and the United States.

Life was so different when my husband was home—full of action and going at high speed. We had a routine when he was at work, and then when he was home, that routine went out the window, like when you are on vacation. We spent every minute together except when I was at work. Although I was happy he was home, I couldn't stop myself waiting for the "other shoe to drop"—getting that dreaded phone call or seeing the other signs that meant he was using again. It is hard living in that situation, always on pins and needles. I trusted God, even though I didn't trust Rich, and I didn't trust myself or my sense of how things were going. Life is funny in many ways. We do everything we can to control things to protect those we love, but we really don't have any influence over many of the events that affect our lives.

Looking back, I see my life as a puzzle. During that time, I couldn't see how my husband's addiction or betrayal fit into my life in a good way. I didn't understand why it had happened or how God could let it happen if He loved me. I know the choices I made that led me to Rich and that place in my life, but now I see the picture that was forming in our lives. We don't realize how these events change us or build facets of our character that otherwise would remain stagnant.

In hindsight, I see how God brought Rich out of alcoholism and addiction. He has been sober now for over twenty years. It took hitting rock bottom for Rich to let go of control and allow God to pull him out of the darkness. He had to give it all to God. It took pain, desperation, and betrayal to see a miracle of rebirth in my husband and our marriage. When you finally face the fact that you don't have any choice or control in the matter, then you move on to relying on God alone to take care of you and to bring you through the dark times, knowing that whatever comes about—it will be what is the best—because God knows what it takes to turn the negative into a positive outcome.

CHAPTER 3

Our relationship with each other and with God grew from that desperate time of alcohol and drug addiction and recovery. It didn't happen overnight, and we had to go through many steps to finally see the healing of our marriage and family. God directed us all the way through. We had financial difficulties stemming from Rich's addictions and treatments that needed payment, and we had to file for bankruptcy. That could have dissolved into a blame game and the end of our marriage, but God kept us on track, and we came through it. We lost our beloved chocolate Lab to a spinal stroke—a heartrending pain on top of all the emotional wreckage of our lives. I drove alone to the veterinary surgery, over an hour away, to pick up her ashes. I sobbed all the way back, holding her next to my heart.

So much loss over the last year overwhelmed my spirit. I had cried every day for more than a year—unable to express my sadness over the events of our first four years together in any other way. God brought me out of a lot of rage and insecurity that comes from living with a profound betrayal of trust. This time in our lives changed me personally, too. I had been a type A personality, always having to be in control. It was not healthy for me physically or emotionally. I was forced to see that thinking I had control over any part of my life or outside events that affected my life was really delusional. I gave everything over to Jesus Christ, and I was content to do so. My trust in God increased as I turned to Him to help me survive both emotionally and mentally. He surrounded me with family and friends who prayed for me. I focused on God, my children, my family, and my job. Throwing myself into everything entirely and trying not to think about the past or the future, I learned to live day-by-day, hour-by-hour.

In early December, Rich called to tell me that he had a couple of days off and was going to go snowboarding with a friend from recovery. I didn't want him to—he was a talented skier but had never snowboarded. He had surfed and skateboarded most of his life and promised to be careful and not get hurt. I was at work when, an hour later, his friend called. "Don't be mad at Rich," he began. "What happened?" I said quietly, knowing it was severe or my husband would have called me himself. "Rich is okay—he was snowboarding down the mountain, and another guy lost control of his snowboard and ran into him." I could barely get the words out, "Where are you?" He replied, "We are at the medics at the base of the mountain, and the ambulance is on the way—he may have broken his collarbone." I could hear Rich in the background groaning, and then he took the phone. "I'm sorry," he said over and over.

Do you know how often I had heard that in the past year? I couldn't even begin to count it, and my first thought in panic was that they would give him a narcotic painkiller, and bam—he would relapse into full-blown drug use again. "I told them not to give me any opiates," he said at once. I was so angry with him. I had told him it was a bad idea to go snowboarding, and he had assured me everything would be fine. He called me again after seeing the emergency room doctor. His collarbone wasn't broken; he had a rotator cuff tear. The doctor said it was a typical injury usually seen in football players. Rich wouldn't be able to use his arm for a while and needed to follow up with an orthopedic doctor. Since he couldn't work, my husband flew back home to see a doctor here.

After returning home and going through physical therapy, Rich and I discussed where he should go in the future—should he keep working in California or apply as a crew boat captain somewhere closer to home. We decided that since he would be gone a month or two at a time for his career and then home for two weeks to a month, it would be better for us if he were closer to home. He applied as a crew boat captain for an offshore oil company near Houston and was hired the same day. We settled into a pattern of Rich at work and Rich at home. He was sober, and our life together as a family was filled with work, activities for the boys, and planning for the future.

We found a local family who had yellow Labrador retriever puppies, and we fell in love with one of the little female pups. We named her Sis, explaining to the boys that she was the only "sister" they would have. She was quite a handful, and Lady, our border collie, tolerated her. Sis, on the other hand, adored Lady. She followed her around and slept right next to her. Lady kept scooting away from her, but that didn't bother Sis. She just rolled over until she could feel Lady against her again. Lady would look at me and sigh, then lay her head down on her paws and go back to sleep. Coco hadn't been big on chewing. Lady had loved to tear up books and shoes when she was young. Sis went above and beyond in the teething category. Nothing was safe from her need to gnaw. We always had a fenced yard and a doggie door to the back so our pets, both the dogs and cats, could go outside as needed. They were house-trained quickly that way, just following the lead of the already-trained pets living in the house.

One day, I came home from work to find Lady waiting at the door for me with a look on her face like—"What in the world did you leave me home with and I didn't do it!" Sis had managed to shred our couch and trailed the

pieces throughout the house, dragging some of it through the doggy door to the backyard until part of it got stuck and wouldn't budge any farther through the opening. Sis was stranded outside, unable to get in because of the debris from the sofa that was lodged in the doggy doorway! She was lying on the porch crying to get in—what a mess!!! The boys and I started picking up the pieces and rolled on the floor laughing—better to laugh than cry—the deed had already been done. Sis knew she was in trouble, but I thought she had been punished enough, locking herself outside for no telling how long. The cats removed themselves from the situation, lolling on the table and watching the crazy dogs and humans drag shredded wood, foam, and cloth through the house.

After saving enough money for a down payment on a house, Rich and I started looking for places to live. He didn't want to buy a house on the island because he refused to have our sons growing up in that "party" atmosphere. He didn't want them making the same mistakes he had made or getting involved in that lifestyle. We found a house that was being built on a golf course in a nearby town, about a twenty-minute drive to the island and about half an hour to the school where my sister and I worked. My father had taught our oldest son to play golf since he was about three years old, and my husband recently began playing. We thought that it would be nice to live where they would be able to enjoy golfing. The neighborhood was gated, so we felt more secure since Rich worked away from home. My parents, my sister, and her husband also lived in the same community, and it was nice to think they would be just minutes away. Our home church had recently completed a new building about five minutes from where we were buying. I could see the church steeple from our backyard. With the move to a new home, a new area, we were starting over.

The boys were excited about the move, and I was happy we would have our own home instead of packing up and going to different rental homes every year or two. My husband was sober, we had a new start in a new home, going to work was like being with family—and we attended church regularly—I even taught Sunday school. Ray was in kindergarten, and Little Rich was in second grade. The boys attended the same elementary school I worked at as a librarian, and my sister taught there. We all four traveled to school together each day: my sister, the boys, and me. It was an excellent time for our family to bond. As we drove to school, we listened to books on CD like *The Lion, The Witch, and the Wardrobe,* by C.S. Lewis, and the rest

of the *Narnia Chronicles,* and the *Harry Potter* series. We talked about our day on the way home while listening to Christian music.

The teachers, administrators, and staff at our school were a supportive "family" of coworkers, encouraging each other, and the boys were part of that. Work was really an extension of our home life. I know it wasn't perfect, but it was a wonderful time. We cared about each other and helped one another in any way we could. I had worked with the same teachers and principal for years, and we had so many connections through our work, our children, and our families. We had all been through so much together: loss of loved ones, celebrations, and graduations, and we helped each other get through the difficult times. The boys played chess, and we traveled with the families of the chess team to state and national tournaments. Our lives were very full—full of activity and full of love. I will always look back on those years as a memorable time, and those people hold a very special place in my heart. I have a connection to them that I haven't had at any other time in my career, and the memories we share are full of love. I know I can't go back to the past, but I am so thankful for that period of my life.

Chapter 4

The front door slammed as the boys came running into the house after finishing their game of horse, bringing me back from my memories of the past. I heard them tell my mother they had beaten Granddad, but I couldn't focus. My mind kept returning to the same questions; Where is he? Is he hurt? Is he alive? I had asked myself these questions often when Rich was in the midst of his addiction and didn't come home. This time, though, it wasn't what Rich was doing to himself that I worried about, but what his kidnappers might be doing to him. We lived near the border of Mexico, and I worked within a half mile of the Rio Grande River. The drug cartels had been in control of Mexico and at war with each other for quite a few years now. We never went across the border anymore, and the news featured stories of shoot-outs and kidnappings daily. Families of kidnapped relatives received body parts and ransom notes, and their hostages were often murdered even after the money was sent. That was my experience with kidnapping, and although Rich's supervisor assured me that the pirates wouldn't hurt my husband and the other hostages because they wanted to receive the highest possible ransom for them, my mind just kept going to what could happen to them and the worst case scenarios haunted me. I also questioned how these pirates could have hijacked the boat with all the protection escorts that were supposed to take these vessels to and from the Agbami oil fields.

I came out of my room, and my mom asked me if I had been able to get any rest. I told her I had napped a little and went into our study to get on the computer. I spent the afternoon searching the Internet for information on hijackings in Nigeria and kidnappings in the country or offshore. I wanted to learn if there was anything in the news about Rich's ship or his

kidnapping. I also wanted to know what had happened to past kidnapping victims in the country and what protocol their kidnappers had followed in their treatment; had they kept them healthy and unharmed to ensure they received the ransom they were asking or did they torture and mutilate their victims, before eventually killing them.

My sister and her husband returned with a parrillada platter of beef and chicken fajitas, sausage, rice, beans, and guacamole for the boys, themselves, my parents, and me for dinner. I managed to choke down a cup of beans, but that was all I could eat that day. Everyone left as the day ended, and the boys changed into pajamas. I was worn out from the emotions I couldn't control. My parents had offered to stay the night, but I just wanted to be alone. I put the boys to bed, praying along with them for their dad and the other men's safety and deliverance. Then I went to my room and knelt, asking God to have mercy on my husband and our family. I woke up in the middle of the night, curled up on the carpet where I had fallen asleep praying. Our new kitten, Sukey, was lying next to me.

A couple of weeks earlier, my brother-in-law had been driving into Brownsville, and right next to the cement barrier that divided the highway, he had seen something small and grey huddled out of the wind. He stopped his truck and ran over to see if it was okay. He picked up the ball of fur, and it began meowing, curling up in his hand. He brought the kitten home, but since they already had three cats (one I had found on the road on the way to work one morning), they asked me if I wanted her. I fell in love with Sukey as soon as I saw her. She was so tiny. Our vet said she was about a month old, and we would need to feed her like a baby kitten. I bought a dropper to feed her the liquid food for kittens he had given me. She liked to sleep nestled like a little gray puff of smoke in the nook between my neck and shoulder. During the day, I would find her in my closet, nestled in my pink furry house shoes.

I mention her because the daily demands I had to provide for her to live helped me stay on a schedule and kept me going. I took pictures of her and texted them to my husband as if he could still see them. I called his cell phone and left messages for him. I wanted to hear his voice and feel like I was communicating with him. It helped me feel like I was still in contact with him, that he could listen to my voice and knew I loved him. I thank God that He held our family in His hands. I didn't know what was happening or what would happen, but I knew He was our rock. He had already brought us through so much; I knew He would get us through this. It is tough to be in

CHAPTER 4

a place in your life where you have absolutely no control or influence over significant events that affect you or the ones you love. You can't save or keep them from harm or pain, but God can. He can save us, and He is there with us through everything. He already knows what will happen, and the things we go through in life help prepare us for those times.

Early the following day, the phone rang in the computer room. I saw the Nigerian Embassy number on the caller ID. I still didn't understand why the Embassy had called me the first day to tell me about Rich's kidnapping. I would have expected to hear from Rich's supervisors first. I listened to the same gentleman's voice that I had spoken to yesterday. I was confused about exactly who this man was on the phone and why he was calling me. He asked me if I had heard from my husband's company. I answered quietly, "Yes, It's true. Rich's boat was hijacked, and he and two other men aboard were taken." He responded, "I'm so sorry, ma'am. We heard that they were taken by MEND."

I had never heard of the organization he was talking about. I asked, "Who is MEND? I don't know who or what that is." He went on, "It's a militant group calling itself the Movement for the Emancipation of the Niger Delta. They have become increasingly active against the Nigerian Army, attacking oil fields, hijacking ships, and kidnapping oil workers. They are armed and violent, but if they have kidnapped your husband and the others, they are after money from the company he works for and should contact them soon."

He gave me his name and phone number so I could call him if I had any questions or needed him to try to contact anyone in Nigeria for me. As I hung up the phone, I thought, is this even real? Yesterday, I was getting ready for work. Today, I am talking, for the second time, to an official of the Nigerian Embassy about a militant group that hijacked my husband's boat and kidnapped him! I wondered also why he was being so helpful—was he trying to get information from me—I didn't know anything. It was such a disconnect from our normal everyday life, and my stress level was so high—I could feel my heart racing through my chest. Our oldest son entered the room and saw me sitting in the computer chair with my hand still on the house phone, staring into space.

I heard his voice from a distance, "Are you okay, Momma, who called?" I answered him woodenly, not thinking about what I was saying. "It was the man from the Embassy in Nigeria who called yesterday. He told me that they think a militant group in the Niger Delta took Daddy,

Tim, and Antonio and that they will contact Daddy's company to ask for a ransom." Little Rich put his hand on my shoulder and replied, "Come on out into the living room," he said. "No, I should stay here by the phone because your dad's supervisor is supposed to call this morning, and I don't want to take a chance that I will miss it," I replied adamantly. He went on, "Okay, let me get another chair then, and I will come in here with you. I don't want you talking to these people by yourself." Ray, our youngest son, had followed behind Little Rich. He added, "Yes, Momma, one of us needs to be here with you." I was touched and proud that our sons, even at their young ages, were offering support and help. We prayed for Daddy, Tim, and Antonio to come home unharmed.

We had just finished praying when the phone finally rang again. Even though it was only 8:30 a.m., I felt like I had been waiting for hours. I saw on the caller ID that it was my husband's supervisor. I took a deep breath to calm myself and put the phone on speaker so the boys could hear, too. I didn't even let him say hello before I asked, "Have you heard anything?" "The hijackers made contact," he said. "They haven't told us their demands yet, just that they have Richard, Tim, and Antonio. Then they let our office manager in Nigeria talk to Captain Tim on the phone so he knows all three men are okay." I closed my eyes. "Thank you, Lord," I whispered. He continued, "I will be meeting here with our company's owner, and we have an international hostage negotiator flying in this morning that we will be working with. He will probably want to talk to you and the other men's wives. I will be locked in meetings most of the day, so I have arranged for a company liaison to communicate any new information we receive on your husband." I thanked him for calling me. As soon as I hung up the phone, the boys ran to open the door. My parents and my sister and brother-in-law had arrived. I gave them the updates and called Rich's parents again to let them know that the kidnappers had made contact but no demands.

I went in to take a shower and fell apart there. I sat down on the tile floor and let the water stream over me as I cried. Trying to keep it together when I was around other people was hard, and I prayed all the time for Rich's safety. After showering, I got dressed and ate a piece of toast. That was about all I could get down. My stomach was churning up acid, and anything I swallowed felt like it was going to come right back up. I sat in the kitchen nook, close to the computer room, so I would have quick access to the landline phone. My sister laid out a puzzle to work on the table so we could keep ourselves occupied during the wait for calls and information.

CHAPTER 4

Around noon, I received a call that surprised me, although I don't know why. I should have expected it. I just didn't realize the FBI would get involved. They identified themselves on the phone and asked if they could send their local agents to meet with me. I agreed, and they asked me to explain how I was notified about my husband and what information I had on the hijacking. I still don't know how they knew about my husband's kidnapping, but I had no problem giving them the information I learned. I just felt uncomfortable giving it to them over the phone, so I answered, "I will tell your agents what I know, but since you all called me and I don't really have any proof to verify your identity, I would rather go over everything with you all in person." "Alright, we understand—they will be in contact," the agent replied, and I hung up the phone. An hour later, the phone rang again; our state Senator called to check how I was doing and if I needed anything from him. I have no idea if they notify these people or who contacts people in cases of kidnapping. The only call I really wanted was the one that would tell me my husband was alive and coming home.

Late in the afternoon, I got a call from the employee liaison from Rich's company. He identified himself and explained that they wanted to keep me updated. They had received another call, but the kidnappers had yet to give them any information or make a ransom demand. They did get to speak to all three men, who were alive and unharmed. I was so relieved to know Rich was well and they had actually heard his voice. He told me the hostage negotiator would also be calling to talk to me to see if I had any information that he could use the next time the kidnappers called. I told him the FBI had been in touch and wanted to talk to me, too. "That's fine." He asked, "Did you contact them?" "No, I thought you all or maybe the person from the Nigerian Embassy spoke to them," I replied. He continued, "No, we haven't spoken to them, and the man who called you from the embassy hasn't contacted us either." I asked, "Did you all give my phone to Tim and Antonio's wives?" "Yes, I spoke with Tim's wife this morning. She said she would phone you," He replied.

I hoped to speak to Tim's wife since she was from Nigeria. I thought her family living there might be able to give us more information about what was happening, or they might have heard rumors of the hijacking and know what group was holding our husbands. About thirty minutes after we hung up, Tim's wife called. She was worried just as I was. She was unsure that our husbands' employers would be able to pay the ransom and ensure the men's safety. She knew of the dangers involved when someone is

kidnapped in that area of the world and what would happen if the captors were angered or their demands weren't met. She had asked her family to find out anything they could about the men being taken hostage. She and Tim had a young daughter. She hadn't told her about her father's kidnapping yet. We agreed to keep in touch and keep each other informed if we heard anything. It was good to talk to someone in the same situation I was, although it wasn't very reassuring to listen to some of the things that could happen if the kidnappers weren't paid.

Another day had gone by without much information. The boys stayed close to me, but I told them to go outside and play basketball or skateboard. They needed to get some fresh air, and I didn't want them worrying about me as well as their father. My parents, sister, and brother-in-law helped take their mind off of what was happening. I worked some on the puzzle, took a long soak in the bath, and lay down to try to rest. I didn't eat much, but I hugged Sis and Molly, our dogs, cuddled Sukey, and drew comfort from my prayers and faith in God. I read some chapters of the Bible and listened to some of our favorite Christian songs as I drifted in and out of sleep with Sukey lying on my shoulder. I awoke to hear my mom fixing dinner and went into the kitchen to help. The phone rang, and I ran to answer it. The call was from an FBI agent, and we set up a time for them to talk to me the following day. I didn't know what I could tell them since I didn't have any concrete information, but maybe they had learned something from their contacts to help me understand what was happening. We finished the day as we started, by having a family prayer for my husband's safety and for all three men to make it home.

I awoke early the following day, shivering as I saw the sun barely rising through the window. I had dreamt that I was searching in the dark for Rich and crying out his name, but I couldn't find him anywhere. I was mentally and emotionally exhausted from lack of sleep and worry. I got down on my knees and cried out for God's mercy on my husband and on us. I lay there focusing on God, remembering His goodness to us in the past and what He had brought us out of. After I calmed down, I got up, showered, fixed breakfast for the boys as they watched cartoons, and fed the dogs and Sukey. Then, I began researching on the internet for any possible leaks of information on the hijacking of Rich's ship from the offshore oilfields of Nigeria, but I found nothing.

I got an email from one of Rich's company's human resources people. She was very caring and wrote that the whole town was praying for the return

of the men. She said the church had met to hold a special prayer service for the men and that the company was there for us. She asked us to let her know if there was anything we needed at all. I appreciated all of the support that they were giving us, and my family and friends were reaching out to others for prayer for Rich and for us. Friends texted and emailed me throughout the day with love and prayers. Everyone was very good at respecting our privacy and kept the information off of social media.

Midmorning, I received a call from the hostage negotiator hired by Rich's employers. By this time, I was getting tired of "the no new information" comment from everyone when they called, and I believed they were not telling me everything they knew. The call started with the negotiator explaining that the kidnappers were following the standard procedure for contact and drawing out the request for ransom. He also emphasized the need for privacy and not letting the information get into the media, or the hijackers might try to use the media as leverage or to make a political statement. Then, the men would be in danger of being used as an example instead of returned for the ransom. I agreed and told him we were not interested in publicity but that I found it worrisome that we had not heard of a specific ransom demand.

"For one thing, in hostage negotiations, it is important to not go into every detail with the family members until things are set," he replied. "I see, so are you saying that you have received a specific amount for the ransom then?" I asked. "I am not saying that," he responded. "Have you or any of the other wives heard from the kidnappers or anyone else in Nigeria?" I answered him, "No, the only one I have heard from is the man from the Nigerian Embassy that I reported about earlier, and I did call Rich's boat right after everything had happened and spoke with one of the crew members, but you all have been informed about that also." The negotiator pressed me, trying to get me to remember more that had been said in my conversation with the representative from the Nigerian Embassy. He had me repeat every word I could remember. Finally, I broke down crying, "I have told you everything he said. I can't remember anything else."

My emotions were already in turmoil from the past few days' events, and I was at my breaking point. The negotiator started questioning me again, and I pushed back, "How did this happen anyway—the company supposedly provides armed escorts for their ships to and from the oil fields, so how could pirates get through those and hijack a ship! Were they not out there doing their jobs? Did they put my husband and the other men in

danger? Tell me that." I continued before he could say anything, "I have a meeting with the FBI today, and you had better believe that I will be asking if it is normal to keep information from the families of the kidnap victims. If you are not going to tell me what is happening, I would prefer if the company liaison called me. He seems to be able to tell me more than you." I hung up the phone before he could reply.

I didn't realize my sons had heard me crying as they came up behind me into the room. I wiped my eyes. Little Rich said, "Momma, remember I told you that I want to be with you in here when you get a phone call. Wait for us to come in before you answer the phone." Ray nodded and added, "Don't talk to them by yourself. They keep upsetting you." "That's okay, boys. I am stressed, and I just lost it." Little Rich answered, "No, one of us is going to be here because we don't want anyone upsetting you like this anymore—you have too much to worry about."

I went to my room and prayed for God to help me keep calm. I was just so tired of not knowing anything, and the worst possible scenarios kept coming into my mind. I told myself that the negotiator was only doing his job. He wasn't hired to be pleasant or helpful to the families. He was hired to get the men back home, and that was all that mattered. I heard the phone ring from my room and ran to answer it. Little Rich and Ray came running into the room to be there with me in case I got upset again. It was Tim's wife. "Have you talked to the hostage negotiator?" she sputtered. I could hear the anger in her voice. I told the boys they could go, that it was the wife of one of the other hostages, and they left. "Yes," I answered. Her voice rose in anger, "I just got off the phone with him, and he kept asking me if my family in Nigeria had any members in the militia or militant groups. Instead of telling me what he knew about the kidnappers, he wanted to know if my family had heard anything about the hijacking and hostages." After she had finished, I answered, "I know—I think it is just that we are so tired of being told nothing. We don't know if our husbands are even still alive. I am going to call the company and see if they will give me any answers." We said our goodbyes and ended the call.

I dialed the liaison's number, thinking getting him on the phone would be easier since they were pulling Rich's supervisor in for meetings over the hijacking. He picked up the phone on the first ring. I'm sure he wasn't expecting my impatience. "I don't know why you all are keeping information from us. I just spoke to Tim's wife, and she says you all aren't telling her anything, either. The hostage negotiator called. He kept

CHAPTER 4

questioning me about what I knew from the Embassy in Nigeria. He questioned Tim's wife about what information her family in Nigeria might know. I have gone over that Embassy phone conversation so many times. I am not going to remember anything else. I have been totally upfront about everything you asked me, even though I don't believe you have been honest with me about everything. I have remained quiet, keeping this out of the media as asked. I believe you all are holding back information about the hijacking and the kidnapping. I will discuss the situation with the FBI agents coming to see me. I plan to ask them if it is normal protocol to keep the victims' families in ignorance."

He sat silently before answering, "I will talk to the company owners and tell them your concerns." He continued, "I know you and your family are going through a lot. I am sure the negotiator didn't mean to add to your stress." I sat, waiting for him to continue. He cleared his throat and said, "We have heard from the kidnappers, and they have made their ransom request. Right now, we are working on the details of the trade for the men, but all of that must be kept strictly confidential. For their safety, we won't be releasing any information on dates or times or the amount of the ransom request." Finally, they had actually given me some information. I replied, "Thank you for giving me an honest answer. I understand the need for secrecy, but can you let me know if we are looking at several days, or can I expect something to happen quickly? I have been praying, and I feel like I need to come out to your offices so I can be on the spot if any information comes through or if my husband is released." He didn't speak for a moment. Then he agreed to talk to the owner about it, and we said goodbye.

I had been feeling the need to travel to their headquarters for several days. I wanted answers and for them to know that Rich was more than just an employee. He was a husband, a father, and a son. I wanted him and our family to be real to them, not just a captain on one of their vessels. It was a little while before I heard back from him. "I talked to the owner, and we don't want you to have to make a trip and then just come here and sit in a hotel waiting. Some of our top personnel are going to fly out and see you. They want to talk to you about any concerns you have and give you any help you need. They will be there tomorrow if that's okay with you." "Yes—I would like that—hopefully, they will be able to give me some answers," I replied. I hung up the phone and told my parents and my sister that some people from Rich's company were going to fly here to meet with me the next day.

I also had to get ready to meet with the FBI. They were coming later today. I didn't know if anything I did would make a difference for Rich's return, but I had to try. I couldn't just sit around and cry. I knew the one thing I was doing that would make a difference was prayer. God hears us, and He is listening. He knows what is in our hearts, and He answers our prayers. I never fell into the trap of thinking, Why Rich? Why me? Why us? Why not us? Are we any different or better than any other person who has experienced tragedy in their life? Things happen in life, good and bad. Some things we make happen by our choices, some by the choices other people make that affect us, and some happen because we live in an imperfect world.

We know that we will go through pain, sorrow, and death as humans. We will face trials and fear, but as Christians, we also know that God is always with us—He walks with us. God promises, "Never will I leave you; never will I forsake you" (Hebrews 13:5b NIV). He hears our prayers and petitions. "I have heard your prayers and seen your tears" (2 Kings 20:5b NIV). Sometimes His answer is yes, sometimes no, sometimes wait—We must do our part too. We need to have faith and believe and trust in God because "We know all things work together for the good of those who love God, who are called according to his purpose" (Romans 8:28 CSB). I knew that in my own self and my own strength, I could not get through this, but I also trusted that I would not be on my own and it would not be my strength that brought me through. God's strength would be with me, and His Spirit would be in me, just as He had been there with me during other difficult times of my life.

I lay down to rest while the boys shot baskets in the basketball hoop my husband and my dad had put together for them this past Christmas. They had worked on it secretly, knowing the joy it would bring both our sons. Little Rich and Ray loved playing basketball. I tried to sleep, but my brain would not shut off. I knew I needed to rest, though, because the FBI agents were coming to the house to interview me in a couple of hours. I got up after about an hour, giving up on getting any sleep, and cleaned up around the house, just trying to keep busy with something to keep my mind off of what was happening. The agents arrived a little early, and one of them shot a few baskets with the boys as he walked up to the door. There were two men and a woman, all seemed to be in their thirties, and they were very kind. They showed me their badges and told me they were there to help in any way they could. They asked me to go through what had happened and

how I had been informed of the hijacking. "I got a call from the Nigerian Embassy early on Friday," I began. They were very interested in the name of the person who had phoned and the information he had given me. "We've always wondered how he comes into these situations and what he actually does at the Embassy," they explained. I didn't go into details of my discussions with Rich's company, just a broad overview of their calls and my conversations with the negotiator and Tim's wife. It took quite a while, and they asked me if the kidnappers had contacted me personally and made any demands. Their question jolted me. It hadn't even entered my mind that the kidnappers might call me. I don't know why I hadn't thought about it. I guess because we weren't rich or influential in any way, just an average middle-class family.

"No, they will probably talk to the company representative there in Nigeria. From what I understand, that is the normal protocol in cases of American oil workers kidnapped in Nigeria. We don't know if it's a group after money or a militant group trying to make a political statement," I replied worriedly. The woman nodded and said, "We want to give you a tape recorder and tapes in case the kidnappers call you to make any demands so you can record the conversation." She handed me a small battery-operated recorder with a couple of tapes and showed me how to use it on the phone. "I'm just so worried they will hurt him," I said. One of the FBI men assured me, "The kidnappings we have seen in Nigeria and other African countries are different from the situations you have seen in the news. They usually try to keep their hostages healthy and in one piece so they can get more money for them. They believe anyone damaged is less valuable, and they are going for the maximum amount of money, which is good for the hostage." The female agent concurred, "Yes, and although you might not be contacted, you need to be ready and know what to say just in case. Now, do you know how much money you could get together for the kidnappers if they requested ransom from you?" "No, I haven't even thought about it since I didn't even realize they might try to contact me." "Let's go through some of the things they might ask you so you will be ready if they do call, and I will write them down so you can keep them by the telephone," the third agent added.

"First of all, you need to ask for proof of life—that's Step 1," the female agent said. Another agent wrote everything down on a yellow notepad, "Here are some different ways you can ask:

How's my husband doing?

In order to be in the right state of mind, I need to know that my husband is okay. I need to talk to him on the phone.

Put yourself in my shoes. It's been _____ days since I've talked to my husband. I need to know that he is okay.

I understand what you're saying, but I can't continue until I know my husband is alive and well.

I want to work things out with you but understand I can only work something out with you once I speak to my husband.

I understand what you're saying, but I will talk about payment/demand/money, etc. when I talk to my husband and know he is okay.

Make sure you are recording any phone calls that you see on the caller ID from Nigeria or a foreign country. Do you have the first step down—or do you have any questions?"

"Yes, I think I understand. Just make sure the kidnappers know I won't talk to them unless I speak to Rich and know he is alive and unharmed." I knew my voice was shaky. The whole experience was surreal; I never dreamed I would be talking to FBI agents—getting instructions on how to deal with kidnappers. I was glad they were writing everything down for me because there was no way I would remember what I should say if they called me.

The agent continued, "Okay, let's go to Step 2, finding out their demands. Make sure they are aware that you don't have access to a lot of money and that they need to deal with the company. Let's go over some things you can say if they demand a large ransom:

We're not rich people. Would my husband be working halfway around the world if we were?

I don't know how much I can get at this time—

I haven't been working since this happened. Rich hasn't been working either. I need time to get some money.

I don't have any money; you'll have to talk to my husband's company about that.

I want to work with you, but we don't have that type of money. The company my husband works for has money.

We are not rich. My husband's company has a lot more money than I do.

CHAPTER 4

*Just because we're American doesn't mean we are rich. We are both
working-class people—we both work for a living—we don't have that
kind of money.*

You see, you can try to deflect them to your husband's company, that they
have much more money to pay than you do, and hopefully, they will then
back off of their demands on you, and they will be dealing with a profes-
sional hostage negotiating situation."

"Yes, first get them to let me talk to Rich and make sure he is okay,
then get them to understand that we don't have a lot of money, and they
should be talking to the company my husband works for if they want to
get a large ransom." I did understand what they were working at. I just
hoped Rich's company would be up for paying the ransom and that the
kidnappers wouldn't get impatient and hurt any of the men while everything was being worked out.

The agent nodded at me, and said, "Alright, the last thing we will go
over is what to say if they threaten to hurt your husband. Kidnappers often
say they will kill a hostage or physically harm them to ensure you pay the
ransom. If they threaten Rich, you can come back with:

*Why would you want to (harm/kill/etc. . . . my husband? He's a good
man. He's a good father and a good person.*

*Rich has always been kind to everyone, especially the Nigerians he
works with on the boat.*

*I want to work with you, but understand there will be no deals if
you harm him.*

*You want money from me. I want him back. If you harm him, you
won't get anything from me.*

*How would killing or hurting Rich make things better or easier for
you? What would that accomplish—then you wouldn't get anything.*

*Do you really want to do that? Do you want his blood on your hands,
the blood of a good man?*

*He's a US citizen. If you kill him, you will get the attention of the
United States government. They will be after you. Do you really
want that?*

*I get angry when you threaten my husband because that won't ac-
complish anything.*

I feel frustrated when you threaten him because I'm trying to work with you on this, but I won't if you harm or kill him.

My husband is a good man. He hasn't done anything to you. Why would you want to hurt him? How would that make things better?

He's never done anything to anyone. He's a good, hard-working man.

Now let's go over everything again—practice turning on the tape recorder before you pick up the phone so the caller can't hear any click or sound from taping them."

I went through the taping process several times. I role-played with one of the agents calling me, pretending to be the kidnappers. I am sure I spoke stiffly, but how would kidnappers expect you to talk if they called demanding money for your husband's life? "I really appreciate you all going through this with me. I hadn't thought of what I would need to do or say if the kidnappers called me," I told them. "We will phone you in a couple of days to see how everything is going, but call us immediately if you hear from the hijackers," they said as they prepared to leave. I watched them drive away from the house through the dining room window. I wondered if I would hear from the kidnappers. At least if they called, I wouldn't be surprised and have no idea what to say to them.

The company liaison phoned that evening. "We are sending some of our people tomorrow morning if that's good for you," he said. "Yes, that's fine. I am not going anywhere. Have you heard anything else about the men—have the kidnappers called back?" He responded quickly, "They have called back, and we are trying to set something up with them. It takes time to make arrangements over there, and our first priority is ensuring the safety and return of your husband and the other men. That's why we want nothing getting out about the negotiations or exchange. Any press could cause everything to fall through. If the hijackers hear they are in the news, they could get scared and kill the men to take care of any witnesses and then run, or they could also try to use the media to spotlight the situation in Nigeria and their political views. Then, the treatment of the hostages becomes secondary, and they could become more violent, playing to the media. Right now, their goal is the ransom money. As long as they know they will only get that payoff if their hostages are healthy and unharmed, they will try to keep them safe to get the money." I took a deep breath, "I understand that. I need to know that everything is being done to bring them home and that negotiations focus on getting them out safely." He assured me they were

CHAPTER 4

moving as quickly as possible, but how could they understand what we were going through? Not knowing what was happening made it more difficult, leaving my mind free to imagine the worst.

It is so hard to get through each day, marking time waiting for phone calls that could bring you the worst possible news or the best. I spent so much time on my knees in prayer or curled up into a ball on my bedroom floor, pleading for God's mercy. Sometimes, I fell asleep, still lying on the floor, only to wake up to my family talking in the kitchen, realizing it was late afternoon or evening. I would cook something for dinner, work on a puzzle with the boys, or try to watch a television show. I felt numb, and things around me grew hazy as I thought about Rich and what could be happening to him. I called Tim's wife, and she called me, too, to see if either of us had heard anything else. I told her the company's people were coming to see me the next day, and she mentioned they were flying in to see her the following day.

The next day, the liaison from Rich's company and two female employees from the human resources department arrived at the house. The boys went outside to play basketball as I ushered the three into our home. We sat around the dining room table, and I made coffee while they took out some papers they had brought. They introduced themselves. The ladies were so kind, hugging me and telling me how much everyone in the company and their church was praying for my husband, Tim, and Antonio to be released quickly and safely. They reassured me that things were moving along. The company liaison said, "Since we are talking in person and not over the phone, where people can listen in, I can tell you that something is being set up to happen for a trade in the next few days." I was so excited and relieved, and I questioned him for more information. The liaison said he couldn't reveal any details and asked me to refrain from speaking to anyone on the phone about it to keep the information from getting out.

One of the ladies from the Human Resources Department said, "We wanted to make sure that you weren't worried about finances or money, so here is the paperwork to show that we will still be paying Rich's salary now as if he was still on the boat." I looked at her in surprise, replying, "I really haven't even thought about it, but I cannot believe they would do anything different. I cannot imagine that if someone at work on their ship, on the job, is kidnapped, they would not continue paying that person's salary." Honestly, money had not even crossed my mind. Right now, everything but Rich's safety was on the back burner. My brain couldn't concentrate on anything

else. They asked if I had everything I needed for my family, and I again said that my husband's safe return was our only concern.

They could see that my family supported me and that Rich was essential to our lives. I wanted them to know that he was important as a father and as a husband, and I wanted them to see him as a person, not some faceless individual. I felt better after meeting with them, but I knew they had just been sent to see me to calm me down and to keep me from showing up at the company's doorstep. I understood their concern, though. They had to focus on getting the men home and were working with the hostage negotiator to achieve that. I am sure they didn't want to worry about dealing with a possibly abrasive or hysterical wife in their offices who might leak vital information to the press. They didn't know me, so they didn't know how I would react to the situation or what I might do, and I didn't want to add to their problem. Well, really, I didn't care about that. I didn't want to do anything that could jeopardize Rich's release or endanger his life.

Chapter 5

The next day was Thanksgiving. We had decided to have our Thanksgiving dinner after my husband was home. None of us felt like holding a big family celebration while Rich was hostage in Nigeria. This waiting game was wearing me down. I felt so useless, not being able to do anything to help my husband get home or even be involved in knowing what was happening with the kidnappers or their requests, letting other people decide whether my husband would be left to die or the ransom paid to bring him home.

I had expected to hear something from Rich's company contacts on Thanksgiving or the day after, but no news came in. Instead of just waiting for my husband's fate to be determined by the people he worked for, I prayed about what I should do. I gave them a few days, and then I decided to call the owner of the company. I looked up his number and called him that evening. He came to the phone, and I explained, "I am Captain Rich Tarpey's wife. I wanted to call and talk to you about my husband. Everyone from your company who phones me says they are doing everything possible to bring him home. I wanted you to understand how important he is to our children and me." I was barely able to get the words out. Tears were choking my voice as I pushed on, "To you, he is just another employee. You probably haven't even met him, but to me, he is the love of my life and Daddy to two boys. They need him, and I need him. I am not worried about money. I just want him home alive and in one piece. Would he still be there if he was one of your family—your son—your brother? Would you still be negotiating with the kidnappers, or would he be on his way home?" After listening to me quietly, the owner answered, "I am doing everything I can—I am not negotiating on the ransom. We are willing to pay what they ask. We are just

trying to set it up so that no one gets hurt. We thought we were going to have them on Thanksgiving Day, but it fell through. We are working on it again, but making sure they are handed over safely takes time. I will bring your husband home, I promise." I believed him and rang off after telling him I would be heading to his company's headquarters. I couldn't wait here at home anymore. I had felt for a long time that God wanted me to go there, and I knew I shouldn't just stay home and wait.

The following morning, I spoke to my sister and her husband about driving to the company's offices in Louisiana. I had planned to go alone with the boys, but Daniel thought I wasn't in a good enough state of mind to safely drive the distance, and he offered to take us. I was very distracted and focused on Rich and what was going on with him, so I agreed that it would be safer for him to drive us. We decided to set out the next day. My parents offered to stay at the house to take care of the dogs, but we took Sukey since she was so young and required a lot of special care. That night, I packed for the boys and me and got together all of Sukey's food and kitty litter for the trip. We loaded the minivan the following morning and picked up Darla and Daniel at their house. They had a friend stay and take care of their pets. Daniel took over the driving. I sat in the back seat with the boys and Sukey. My mind was all over the place, and I couldn't concentrate. I watched the familiar sights of the Rio Grande Valley go by as we drove north. We live in the southernmost tip of Texas, so it takes about twelve hours of driving to get out of the state. We stopped in Houston to get takeout for lunch, and I phoned ahead to reserve a hotel. I knew we would be getting there late, so I wanted to make sure we had rooms that allowed us to have Sukey.

We were about an hour away from our hotel in Louisiana, driving through the darkness, the highway surrounded by trees dripping with moss, when my phone rang. It was an international phone number, and I thought the Nigerian Embassy was calling again. I answered the phone, and through the static I heard the voice I had only dreamed of for the last fourteen days. "Stephanie, honey, it's me, Rich." My voice raised, and I cried, "Rich, Rich, is it you?—Daniel, pull over somewhere—it's Rich." Daniel pulled over onto the shoulder of the highway. My husband's voice came through, "Yes, babe—it's me—I can't talk because they are getting us to safety, and the other men need to call their families to let them know, too. I love you so much. I will call you back when they get us to the safe house." I couldn't believe it. Relief and joy filled me! I thanked God that

CHAPTER 5

Rich was free. My heart was so full as tears rolled down my face. "They have him," I told Darla, Daniel, and the boys. He just got to the phone to tell me he was going to the safe house. He's free!" I burst out laughing and crying all at the same time. Suddenly, instead of a trip of desperation, our drive became one of celebration. I couldn't believe it! Was it a coincidence that the ransom was paid and Rich and the other hostages were rescued the day after I spoke with the company's owner? I don't know. I do know that God got Rich out of there—that he was safe and alive. I just kept repeating, "Thank You, God!" over and over.

We drove on to the hotel and checked in. I called my parents to let them know that Rich had called and was on his way to a safe place. I told them not to tell anyone until we knew he was leaving the country. Next, I phoned Rich's mother, father, and stepmother to give them the news. We cried in relief together over the phone, and I let them know to make sure they didn't say anything to anyone until Rich was safely in the States. Then we went out for a celebratory dinner. We had been so exhausted from the drive and stress that all we planned to do was get to the hotel, order pizza, and go to bed. After that phone call, I felt rejuvenated, and we all felt like celebrating.

I don't know how to explain the relief that came over me, the weight that lifted from my shoulders, body, mind, and spirit. I actually felt like eating for the first time in two weeks. Rich was alive! I hadn't had a chance to tell him that I was on the road and not at home. We sat around a scarred wooden table and ordered crawfish. I felt like life could go on now. Once I returned to the hotel, I gave Sukey a little treat and fell into bed, exhausted. I didn't think I could sleep because I was so excited, and the boys were bouncing off the walls, but we all went out once our heads hit the pillows.

When I woke in the morning, I spoke to my husband's supervisor, and Rich called me to tell me they had made it to Lagos. He and the other three men had to be seen by a doctor to get checked out and ensure they were healthy enough to travel. They ran blood work on all three to check for malaria and malnourishment. They also ran toxicology screenings. The liaison from the company called me as we were heading to Galliano and told us they had set up a meeting with the men at the airport in New Orleans. They wanted to debrief the men at their office, put us up in a hotel in New Orleans, and fly us back home after a couple of days. I spoke with my sister, Daniel, and the boys, and we discussed our options.

We decided it would be best to meet Rich at the airport and spend time with him. Then, they would drive the boys and Sukey back home while Rich and I returned to his company's office for the debriefing. We checked out of our hotel and then went to New Orleans. On the drive, I called Abby to let her know Rich was coming home. I could hear the joy and relief in her voice as she said she would let the people at work know, too. Darla phoned the school she worked at to let them know. They had been praying for Rich's release, too. We had a while to wait for the flight to get in, so we took the boys to a sidewalk café for breakfast. I had Sukey stashed in my bag, but she kept poking her head out, wanting some breakfast also.

We were all walking on cloud nine, elated because the men were getting home. I was nervous, too, not knowing what had happened to Rich or the other two men and what effect it would have on him. I worried that his kidnappers had given him narcotics and that his sobriety would be affected. After eating, we drove to the airport, and we waited outside the terminal for Rich to arrive. There were signs welcoming the men back, and someone had brought a camera to film their homecoming. I saw the company employees who had come to the house, and I met Tim's wife and daughter. I spotted Rich as he walked toward us. Tears filled my eyes as he came through the gate. He looked so thin, and his face was drawn and haggard, but he was smiling. The boys and I wrapped our arms around him, and then Daniel and Darla joined us in a big family hug. I wanted to stay in that cocoon of relief and love forever.

I told Rich our plan was for the boys and Sukey to go home with Darla and Daniel so we could meet with the corporate people, and then they would fly us home. He agreed that would be the best thing to do. The company rented a car for each couple so Rich and I could drive to their headquarters and then back to a hotel close to the airport. That would be better than riding with their representatives. We wanted time to talk, and I wanted to know how my husband really was. We hugged the boys and my sister and brother-in-law as we told them goodbye. Rich and I walked to the rental car, and I got in on the driver's side. "Alright—how are you really doing honey?" I began. I could tell that he was a ball of nerves. He was jittery and couldn't stop moving. His legs and hands were constantly in motion. "I'm okay—I am just so glad to be back in the United States."

He took out a photo that they had taken after the three men were rescued, and I didn't even recognize him. All three of the men looked emaciated and filthy. They had long, scraggly beards, and their hair strung

down the sides of their faces. They all looked like they had just come out of a refugee camp. "This was at the safe house," Rich said. His voice trembled. "I thought I was going to die, honey. I didn't think I would ever see you or the boys again, but I knew if they killed me, I would be all right because I would be with God. I felt peace about it. The only thing that worried me was whether you and the boys would be okay. I knew my company would provide financially for you all, but I knew how hard you would take it, and I worried about the boys growing up without a father." "Shhhhh," I told him as I pulled the car over and wrapped my arms around him, and he laid his head on my shoulder. "God brought you home alive, and you are back here with us. He delivered you and had mercy on our family. I am so thankful that God made a way for you to come home." I cried as I spoke the words, and we gave thanks together to Christ for bringing him and the other men home.

Chapter 6

We had plenty of time to talk while I drove from the airport to the company headquarters. Rich took out a palm cross and handed it to me. "I made this while I was there—in the jungle," he told me. "God was all that kept me going. I had to put you and the boys away from me, out of my mind. I couldn't think about you all because I had to keep my mind and heart strong and be ready to let go of everything—to let God's will for me be done." "Tell me about it—tell me what happened. How it happened—I thought there were always armed escorts when you all were running." I was full of questions, but Rich needed to tell me in his own words. The following is his account of the events.

November 18th—Day 1:

The day started out as a regular run. We were returning to the dock from the Agbami oil field. Our supply boat was loaded with crude oil. Agbami lies about 220 miles southeast of Lagos and 70 miles offshore of Nigeria in the central Niger Delta. Texaco and Chevron operated under their international companies, drilling and pumping the oil out of Nigeria's most extensive deep-water development. Tim and I were American captains running a platform motor supply vessel. Our engineer, Antonio, was from Mexico, and the rest of our crew was Nigerian. Captain Tim was asleep in his cabin below, and I was on duty. We were en route to the security checkpoint, having left the Agbami field at about 4:30 in the afternoon.

At about 8:30 in the evening, I thought I heard knocking on the back door. The back door to the bridge was locked while the ship was underway according to mandated protocol. Turning to our AB, Able Bodied Seaman,

who was watching the radar, I said, "Hey Mark, who's out on the deck?" Before he could answer, I heard the sound again. I went to the back door to check and looked in shock as a man in a red ski hat carrying a machete and an AK-47 motioned to a bunch of men running up the stairs. They began yelling, "Unlock the door!" Thinking quickly, I said, "I have to go get the key!" I turned to Mark urgently and told him, "Mark—wake up Captain Tim—Now!" Mark ran to Captain Tim's cabin, and I sprinted down the stairs to alert the rest of the crew. Before I was halfway down the stairs, I heard a loud bang—like a gunshot and glass breaking as they shot out the window to get inside the bridge and crew quarters. "Get to the muster stations—now—all hands now!" I yelled to all the crew as I ran past their rooms, knowing that armed men were boarding us.

Antonio immediately started the fire monitor that blasts water. No one was on deck to steer the monitor. We were all scrambling to do anything we could to protect ourselves. Two more crewmembers joined us downstairs in the engine room, and we tried to get a plan together. We started hiding the Nigerian crewmembers in the engine control room, but Antonio and I knew we couldn't hide. They had already seen me. If I hid myself, the other crewmembers would be in danger. The hijackers would search the boat until they found me and hurt or kill the crew to get to me, and I wasn't going to be responsible for someone's death to save myself. Antonio felt the same way. We both got down on our knees in the engine room and put our hands up over our heads, waiting for the hijackers to make their way down. I don't know what was going on in Antonio's head, but I was praying to God to bring us out of this unharmed.

My thoughts kept flashing back to the last time I saw my wife and boys. She was crying as she left me at the airport to fly out for this two-month hitch, and I remembered wrapping my arms around her and the boys as she prayed for safe travels and my return. I always left a note for each of them; this time, I left an anniversary card for my wife. I had been in satellite phone range on our anniversary, so I called to tell her I loved and missed her.

I pulled my mind back to the present—Stop this, I told myself. You have to focus on survival right now. About fifteen minutes had passed when one of the militants stormed into the engine room waving a machete and his AK-47, shouting, "Give me your gold chains, watches too." He pointed to me and said, "That gold ring—take it off—give it to me!" I removed the ring and told him, "This is my wedding ring. It was blessed by a minister

when my wife and I were married." "Keep it," he grunted. "Take off your shoe and put it on your toe, or someone will take it." I took my ring off and, lifting my foot out of my shoe, shoved it on my toe. I crammed my foot back into my shoe. He searched our pockets and removed a knife from Antonio. Then he grabbed us both, roughly jerking us up. "Lock arms together and hold onto each other's shirts," he directed as he marched us up the stairs to our staterooms. I looked in dismay as we were shoved into my cabin. It was torn apart. Everything from my backpack was dumped onto the floor. My clothes were tossed all over the room, muddied from the boots that had trampled around the area. "Money—I want whatever money you have," he demanded. I searched my pack to see if anything was left in it. "They already took it all—see—nothing's left." I showed him the empty pack. I found some phone cards that had been tossed aside and offered them to him, so he took those. Two more hijackers crowded into the stateroom. They were anxious to get in on stealing our valuables. They grabbed my television and computer.

Shoving his gun into our backs, the hijacker marched us to Antonio's room, and the whole process started again. Of course, they had already tossed his room as they had mine and taken all the cash he had stashed in his room for emergencies. Antonio found a bunch of phone cards and gave them to the guys, and they piled up his electronics to take as well. After taking all they wanted from our rooms, Antonio and I were forced upstairs into the wheelhouse. I saw the glass window busted out from the gunshot when they had forced their way in, and then I saw Captain Tim face down on the floor. "Get down on the floor with Capo. Put your heads down," one of the hijackers shouted, threatening us with their machetes. "Give us all your phones, NOW!" he yelled, as we didn't move quickly enough. One of the men collected our phones while the others used their machetes to destroy the ship's radios. "Where are we? What's your position?" They questioned us. We were surprised that they didn't know our location. We answered as best we could, giving our last known offshore location. Grabbing up Captain Tim, two hijackers yanked him down to his room. Antonio and I stayed on the floor, kneeling among the broken glass.

Although they weren't gone long, it felt like a lifetime waiting for them to bring Tim back upstairs. When they returned, Tim held a bag full of his clothes. As they walked him to the back door, I felt the hard metal of a gun tap my back, and one of the men dragged me up off the floor. They put the gun to my head as they shoved me through the back door after

CHAPTER 6

Tim. I heard Antonio stumbling through the shards of glass on the floor as he was escorted outside on the deck along with Tim and me. When we reached the back deck, they shoved life jackets into our hands—"Get these on now." We saw the pilot ladder hanging over the side of the boat and a small speedboat they had used to get offshore and board our ship. "Get in," one of the men said as he forced us to climb down the ladder and into their small craft. They looked around in confusion, and we overheard them discussing our position, "Where do you think we are—how do we get back to the camp—I don't know."

The two men, who seemed to be in charge, took Tim back up to the deck of our motor vessel to get a better sight of our location. Antonio and I stayed on their speedboat with five of their men. They pulled their boat around to the back of our vessel and threw a line off the bow. The others tied the rope, attaching their craft to the stern of our supply vessel. As we got underway, the speedboat in tow began to vibrate. Antonio and I looked at each other—the smaller boat we were in couldn't handle the speed as the water crashed against its sides, threatening to break it apart. "Slow down!" our captors in the boat with us shouted over the sound of the vessel's engines, "We're going to break up!" The ship's engine noise lessened as Captain Tim pulled back on the speed.

We ran for about three hours, traveling about eight knots toward shore. The men on the little speedboat untied the ropes, attaching us to our supply vessel. Then they pulled alongside to pick up the other hijackers and Captain Tim. Heading side-sea at full speed, we ran towards the coast. Two men were up on the bow, watching for an opening off of the river the men planned to use to travel to the jungle's interior. After we had gone quite a distance, they gestured that they had found the entrance to the river, and we turned in and headed upstream using a flashlight to help navigate in the darkness. Sliding through the water on the winding river as we went deeper into the Niger Delta, we began to see lights. "Get down on the floor now!" the hijackers barked. Looking out above the side of the boat, I saw what looked like a group of people with spotlights shining on us as we went by. We passed several more camps as we continued up the river.

We stopped to refuel from some spare drums of fuel they had stored on the speedboat. I guess our captors decided they were safe at this point because they started talking to us, not just shouting out orders. One man asked, "Your Company has money—will they pay money for you?" That gave us a feeling of relief that they had kidnapped us for ransom, not to

make a political statement. If they wanted money for us, we would at least be valuable to them, and they would be less likely to torture or kill us. "Yes, they have money—they will pay to get us back, but only if we are unharmed," we assured them as they refueled the boat and started back up the river. This time, we were allowed to stay sitting up.

When we got thirsty, our captors gave us bottled water to drink that they had taken from the supplies on our motor vessel. They even gave me a pair of coveralls to wear since I was getting cold. We ran for about another hour, traveling deeper into the Niger Delta. They didn't use any GPS or guidance system, so we wondered how they knew where we were. We came to a stop after they found an opening in the mangroves. Using a flashlight to guide the boat driver, we slipped through and came to rest on a little piece of land. This was their hideout. As we looked around in the dark, surrounded by water, mangroves, and jungle, we realized we were totally in their power. No one would find us out here. No one would know our location to rescue us, and we had nowhere to run except the jungle.

Our captors climbed out of the boat and began unloading their supplies—food, drugs, and alcohol. Then they started hauling out everything they had taken from our motor vessel—televisions, computers, bags of clothes, water, anything that would bring them money or that might be needed while they hid out with us—their hostages. Two of the men gathered wood and started a fire. A few others set up a pole to get cell phone reception.

The hijackers ordered us to stay in the boat while they made preparations on the island. They finally allowed us to talk to each other since we weren't passing other people on the river who might hear us. "We were seventy miles offshore—how did they get to us out there—why did they take us?" I began asking. Tim continued my thoughts, " I thought our company paid money to protect all of us and their vessels." We still didn't know who the hijackers were, if they were a small group by themselves, or if they were one of the organized militant groups. We just knew they wanted money. Antonio sat there, not saying much, just watching our captors closely and listening to see if any of their cell phone calls were going through. We could tell they weren't having any success—there didn't seem to be much signal, even with the pole they had set up.

Still sitting on the boat in the dark, we could see around the fire that the men were taking some drugs and had started drinking moonshine, or kai-kai, as they called it. They seemed to be celebrating, but you could tell they

CHAPTER 6

were high and acting wild, waving their arms around and dancing about. It looked like some of them were acting out their "bravery" on our supply vessel and how they had taken us. As the sun rose, we could hear the sound of machetes swishing through branches. The rest of the men slept around the smoking fire, splayed out from their binge during the night.

After the sun had been up about an hour, the sound of the machetes stopped, and we heard footsteps crunching through debris as a few men approached the boat. "Come," they called and motioned for us to follow. They led us about fifty feet to a makeshift hut. They had used their machetes to cut down tree limbs and palm fronds. They placed two larger limbs on the ground and covered them with smaller branches to build up a small platform off the ground. Using thick tree limbs for poles, the men had raised a roof out of the remaining branches and palm fronds. They had built a place to keep us undercover. "Sit, are you hungry?" they asked. We nodded, and they brought us some of the bottled water they had taken from our vessel and some food they had prepared. They left us alone while we ate. Trying to get the food down as stomach acid rose in our throats from fear and nerves, we looked around to see what we were in for.

We were on a small piece of land that was high enough to remain uncovered when the fresh river water rushed in on the incoming tide. We realized there was no chance of us running off anywhere. There was nowhere to go, and we had no idea of our location or what was out there in the Niger River Delta. We looked up, wondering if we could be spotted from the air, but the limbs of the trees were dense, making a canopy that covered us, and I doubted even the campfire could be seen. One of the men came over and took our plates as we finished eating. Two others started building a fire. "How come you are building up a fire?" I continued, "It's already getting hot." One of the men answered, "We will keep the snakes away. "Don't go walking around too much. Poisonous snakes are everywhere here, some on the ground, some in the trees." Tim, Antonio, and I looked at each other. Great, nowhere to go, and if someone did get bit by a snake, that would be it—I'm sure they wouldn't be running us to a hospital for anti-venom.

Now, it seemed all we had to do was wait. My body needed rest, but my mind began to wander—how did I get to this point? How could this happen? I came back to reality and heard our captors laughing and joking around. They had started drinking kaikai again, and the partying continued. Sometime in the afternoon, two of their men left in the boat. We didn't know where they were going, but we overheard some of the others talking and

thought from what they said that we were close to Bonny Town. We didn't know how far away it was, but we knew there were a lot of Americans there because most of the oil companies had compounds based in the area.

As we sat in our jungle hut with two thin foam mattresses, a mosquito net, and two sheets, we realized they planned for us to be there for a while. We could hear a helicopter flying overhead. We looked out around the roof of the hut. Peering through the tree branches, we saw it was an oil rig flight. They wouldn't be looking for us yet. We didn't even know if they were aware that our supply vessel had been hijacked and we had been kidnapped. As the sun went down, they ordered us to get under the net and stay there so we would not get bitten by mosquitoes.

Lying quietly in the darkness, we heard them talking. One man boasted, "We are gonna get some big money for these boys—yes—big money—American money—oil money." Another man laughed, adding, "And if the boss don't pay—we cut off their heads and chop their feet off—then we will drink their blood so we will be protected." They kept talking about the same thing: money or our blood—I couldn't tell which one they wanted the most. The man who seemed to be in charge came back and told them to be quiet, "Shut up—we need to keep them from getting sick or hurt so we can get the ransom. We did this for the money." Then he brought us Tim's medicine bag they had grabbed from his room. The three of us took the doxycycline, our antimalarial medication. They also set up four fuel cans around us and lit them on fire. They could watch us better with the firelight to make sure we didn't try to escape, and the fire also helped repel the insects and snakes. I prayed that all three of us would make it out of this alive. Finally, we went to sleep—the first day was over.

November 19th—Day 2:

We woke up to loud, jarring music and the sounds of partying. Our captors were already drinking—I don't know if they had ever stopped. We could smell the smoke from the pot, Indian hemp, as they called it. We got up, and they gave us two cans of fruit cocktail for breakfast. The fire had gone out, so I started collecting some wood to get it going again. "Sit down—we will get the wood. You don't walk around." I don't know if they were worried I would make a break for it or that I might step on a snake. They got wood for us and started the fire back up. We made a little pile of

plastic bottles and collected some green leaves so we could put out the fire in case it caught our hut alight.

We didn't have a watch, so we went by the sun to try to judge the approximate time. Sometime around noon, they called Tim over to make a call. The leader, who they called Capo, said, "Phone the boss—time to talk." Tim didn't know the number of the Nigerian office. "I have the office number on my laptop—you all have it here," I told them. They started shuffling through the belongings they had taken from the boat. "It's the one with the apple on it," I called out. One of the men brought me my laptop and barked at me, "Here, find the number." I opened up my computer and saw my wife's picture that I had as the screen saver. I closed my eyes and tried not to think I might never see her and our sons again. I focused on the moment and prayed silently for God's strength and that He would bring us through this.

I found the number, and one of the men typed it into the phone contacts. He took the phone and handed it to Capo. The guy who brought me my computer returned to get it, and I asked him, "Can I wipe it?" He looked confused and asked, "What's that mean?" I answered, "It means I will take everything off it and leave it like new—blank. If anyone finds it, they won't know that you took it from me, so they won't know you were one of the kidnappers." He looked at me real hard and then said, "Yeah—good—I like that—take everything off." I was relieved because I didn't want them to have access to photos or information about my family or home.

As I opened the photo files on my laptop, I felt a tight ball well up in my chest. I looked at pictures of our summer road trip to Yosemite, the boys when they were younger, and my favorite photos of my wife. I tried to hold back the tears as I clicked the mouse and moved each one to the trash icon. It felt as if I was saying goodbye to them and would never see them again, never know their laughter or their hugs. I had to face then that I might not see the boys grow up, and I knew the desperation and pain Stephanie would feel when she found out I was gone. I realized then that I had to focus on God and getting out of this, not on my family and my love for them because that would undo me.

I saw the playlist of my favorite Christian songs that I had saved on my laptop. I turned the volume low so only I could hear it and pressed play. The music reminded me exactly what I needed to remember: that Jesus Christ was with me. His hand was on my shoulder. "For He Himself has said, I will never leave you, nor forsake you" (Hebrews 13:5b NKJV). I truly know He is my Savior, and I prayed for Tim and Antonio to have the same comfort. I

prayed for my family and the pain I knew they were going through. Most of all, I prayed for God's ultimate will. If He wanted me in heaven, I would be honored, willing, and blessed to go. Fear and anxiety came when I thought about my wife and our boys and how they would get through this.

While I was working on my laptop and praying, our kidnappers had been trying to get a phone signal. They finally got through to our office in Nigeria. We listened as Captain Tim spoke to the base operations manager. Tim tersely relayed the information that the men told him to say about our kidnapping and that they were holding us hostage. The manager asked, "What do they want? What are their demands?" Tim repeated the question to Capo. He demanded, "200,000,000 naira—you have two days to get the money, or your men are dead." After that statement, Capo hit the end call button on the phone.

Tim came back over to Antonio and me, and we asked him if they had said anything that we couldn't hear, but he said no, they had kept the call short. "Okay, now we know what they want," Antonio said. We added the amount after going through the money change with Nigerian currency. We came to about $155,000 in US dollars. We knew that shouldn't be a problem for our company to come up with. Antonio said, "No, that's not right—it's not $155,000." We sat down, worked it out again, and realized he was right—the correct exchange would be almost 1.5 million US dollars. My heart plummeted. We didn't know if our company had that much cash available, and to come up with that in two days and get into Nigeria was impossible. It didn't look good for us. It was a waiting game. The operations manager would contact the company's main office in Louisiana, and the ball was in their park. They would have to decide whether to pay the ransom or leave us to die.

Sitting around, waiting, and hoping for the phone to ring all day was nerve-wracking. We didn't eat any lunch, just had some ramen noodles later for dinner. We had little to talk about. Our minds centered on listening for the sound of a cell phone ring, but nothing, no phone call. The sun started sinking in the sky, and with it went the warmth of its light. Tim, Antonio, and I went into the hut and got on our bed under the mosquito netting. We lay there and listened as the pirates talked about juju and wearing their protection bands made of red and white beads. They stayed drunk and high twenty-four hours a day, and we didn't feel very protected from them, even though they would get more money if we were unharmed. They were ranting about different ways to escape after getting

the ransom. Then they went on about the best way to kill us and leave our bodies for the animals to eat. Lying there, in the hot, humid air of the Nigerian jungle, while our captors chanted voodoo spells and laughed about our deaths and the feast the animals would have on our bodies, I tried to sleep but just fell into uneasy dreams, thinking of what my wife and sons were doing and if they knew about the boat hijacking yet.

November 20th—Day 3:

We woke early from a restless, noisy night. Our captors were partying again and getting jacked up on their moonshine. They were cocky at the thought of all the money they would get for us. The witch doctor had arrived at the camp, and that increased our fear that they might use us in some ritual or harm us so they would earn protection. They talked of making amulets from our body parts and bloodletting. I prayed for God's strength. I knew that if I did die, I would be with Him, which comforted me as long as I could keep my mind off those I would leave behind.

One of the men brought over some moldy bread for our breakfast and some tea. We picked the mold off the bread and split it between us. Our sleeping arrangements were getting to us, as was the anxiety and fear over whether we would be killed or survive. The platform they had made for our bed was not very big. Our feet hung off the end, and we had to lie on our sides so the three of us could fit, but no one was going to take the chance of sleeping on the floor with the poisonous insects and snakes. After breakfast, we decided to rest so we could talk more privately than sitting apart in the hut. We whispered back and forth, discussing how to improve our situation. Finally, we decided to throw some of the empty plastic water bottles on the fire to blacken the smoke. Hopefully, a helicopter flying by might see it.

We had nothing to do with our time but wonder and worry about what was happening with the ransom, how our families were, and if we would make it out of this alive. We were starving and thirsty. They gave us a few bottles of water, but we didn't know how much water they had, so we rationed it carefully between us. They were drinking straight from the river. There was a slimy sheen on the river water, and who knows what it was. The men would move it off the top, scoop up the river water underneath, and drink it. I hope they didn't make our tea with that. It was even more

disgusting because they bathed and urinated, even relieved their bowels in the same area of water they used for drinking.

Later that afternoon, they let us walk around the area. They realized there was nowhere for us to go to escape. We got up off our little perch and stretched our legs. It felt good to move around. They didn't bring us anything to eat the rest of the day. We could hear them talking to each other. They were questioning why it was taking so long for our people to call back about the money. They realized the cell phone didn't get a good signal where they were keeping us and decided they may have to take us with them later to find a place with better reception.

Two of the men left in the small boat. They returned a couple of hours later with bottles of gin, kaikai, more marijuana, and whatever kind of pills they were taking to start the party all over again. We sat worrying, hoping they didn't get so messed up that they would harm us. We also talked about what we would do if we made it out of this and how we wanted to do things differently in our lives.

I had already turned my life over to Jesus Christ back in 2000 when I got sober, so I knew that even though we were in a bad situation, God had a plan for my life. I had to be okay with whatever might happen, even if that meant that I died at the hands of our captors. I have never been one to sit around and wait, so I decided to surround myself with Christian symbols. I wanted these people to know that they did not have control over what happened to me, whether I lived or died, that Jesus Christ was in command of my fate. I began picking up small sticks and gathered palm fronds. Some of the men looked at me curiously, but they soon turned back to their partying when they saw I wasn't trying to escape.

I made crosses out of the sticks and placed them in the ground all around our little makeshift hut. I had found some small rope and used it to make a cross and necklace, which I wore around my neck. I also made crosses out of the palm fronds and laid them around with the stick crosses. One of the men came walking by me, and I handed him a cross. I said, "Here you go, you need this, and Jesus loves you." He looked at me like I was crazy and said, "How can you give me this. You know that I may have to kill you." I felt such peace when I replied, "The only way any of you can kill me is if God allows it, and if that is what God allows you to do, I am okay with that because I will be going home to my Father in heaven." I really think this messed with his head. To hear people sitting around talking about killing you as if it were a normal, matter-of-fact

conversation was terrifying. They didn't think any more of killing us than of killing an insect. Life had no value to them, and our lives only had value if they could get money for us.

Later, the hijackers started offering us drinks of their kaikai. They chanted, "You drink! You drink, or we hurt you!" Tim and Antonio each took a sip, but I refused to taste it. I knew if I even took a little drink, it would destroy my sobriety. God had brought me too far out of the near-death of addiction and alcoholism that there was no way I would go back into that life. "You can kill me, "I told the men, "But I will not drink any of your kaikai, and I won't smoke any of your weed. It would be better for me to die than to do that." Capo stepped in and told them to leave me alone. He threatened the partiers, telling them he would kill them if they did any-thing to keep him from getting his ransom money from our company. That seemed to sober them up a little, although they did shoot us angry looks and threatened what they would do if the company didn't pay up.

Although I wouldn't drink anything, I did start smoking again. I had given up cigarettes a while back, but when Tim brought out the ones he had on the boat, I smoked some to help calm my nerves. It was driving me crazy, not being able to do anything but sit around and think about what might happen. I prayed and sang Christian songs to myself. I prayed for God's will to be done and for Him to take care of my family. I thanked Him for bringing me out of the life I had been living and for giving me a life of sobriety and love.

We went to bed early because we had to be under the netting in our hut by evening so we would have less chance of getting malaria from the mosquitos that swarmed the area after dark. Even though we took the an-timalarial medication, we were still concerned about getting sick. We were so hungry since we hadn't eaten anything besides the moldy bread, and our stomachs were rumbling. We lay there on our cots until we eventually nodded off from sheer exhaustion.

November 21-Day 4:

Early in the morning, we heard loud yelling and a scraping noise. Our kid-nappers were sharpening the axe they had taken off our vessel and seemed to be chopping some oddly shaped pieces of wood. They got all three of us up and brought us over to the fire. Our captors chanted, "Watch—you watch—you see—all three of you—You see!" The witch doctor, who was

third in command of the operation, chopped the wood and then sharpened the axe again. Then he swept the axe at the wood to see how far it could cut through the logs in one swoop. He kept sharpening the axe and testing it until he could halve the wood in one fell swoop.

While he was testing the axe, we saw how messed up he was. His eyes were large and red, glaring through the puffy, swollen skin that covered his face. "Look—see—do you know what he is doing?" they asked us. We shook our heads. I didn't really want to know. "The wood is like human knees, your knees! He can cut off your lower leg and feet for the blood to gush out for sacrifice. We will eat the flesh to get your power," they cackled. Finally, the witch doctor spoke, "You don't believe—watch!" He grabbed Antonio by his shoulder and tried to take a bite out of his arm. Capo yelled, "Hey, stop!" and grabbed the man. "You kill him, and there will be no money. I'm in charge! You do what I say!" You could see the tooth marks on Antonio's arm, and he was really shaken up. We knew that these men could easily kill us and make our bodies disappear—if Capo weren't there to keep control over them.

They didn't give us any breakfast that day. I don't think Antonio could have eaten if they had. A couple of hours later, they brought over a can of beans and two bottles of water for us to share for the whole day. We were thirsty, but we definitely were not going to drink the water in the river. I continued working on the crosses that I was making from the palm fronds and praying for God to keep evil from us.

It was so hot and humid, and we had not bathed in four days. I had finally had enough, got up, walked towards Capo, and asked, "Do you have any soap. I need to wash up. I feel filthy, and we smell bad." He laughed and said, "Thank you! You guys stink!" Then he handed me soap and made his men take us a little way upstream to another area of the river to bathe, a place that had not been used as a toilet. I took off my clothes and waded into the river. Using the bar of soap, I cleaned the filth of the last four days off of my skin. Boy, it felt good! After I got out, Tim decided to bathe, too. He grabbed the bar of soap and walked into the river.

The three of us talked a lot about our situation. We realized that we couldn't start feeling sorry for ourselves. That path would lead us to a pit of darkness. We had to keep ourselves up, looking for ways to escape, if possible, ways to protect ourselves and to keep the hope of going home alive. We were in a desperate situation and had no control over what would happen to us, but we did have control over how we reacted to the

CHAPTER 6

threats and the danger. Fear can kill you. It can eat at you and drive your mind into a cycle of desperation, causing you to do stupid things that could get you killed.

Our captors started drinking heavily early in the day and began complaining, "I want to see my woman and my kids," one of the men yelled. The others started getting angry and hollering that they wanted to go home to their villages and see their families. "We've been gone too long! This is taking too much time. You said just a few days. People are talking about three kidnapped Americans. They will figure we are part of it since we haven't been home. They are going to go after our families." The men continued working themselves up, and then some of them started in on Capo.

We listened to them grumbling about how he didn't have anything to worry about because he was a Captain in the Nigerian Navy. He had taken time off of work so they wouldn't be looking for him. They called the second in command, Sonny, and we overheard them talking about his position in the Nigerian Army as a sergeant. They said he had taken leave also. We were shocked that the two leaders of the militant group were in the Nigerian military. From what we had been told, they were hired to protect our boats and the fuel drilling platforms. What were they doing, hijacking and kidnapping the crew from ships they were supposed to be protecting?

The phone reception had gotten worse, and Capo said they would have to run down the river to get a good signal so they could contact our company again and find out what was taking so long. Later that evening, two of the men left and came back with something that looked reptilian. Antonio saw them and said, "Hey, they got some lizards." "No, those are gators or crocodiles," I answered him when I had a better look. Some of the others got out their knives, began skinning them, and took out some of the organs. "I cannot eat lizards," Antonio grimaced. "I can, I'm starving to death!" I said. The two men who had cleaned the gator began cooking it up over the fire and mixed in a few snails. They brought us some, and Tim and I both wolfed it down.

I asked, "Who can cook Agusi soup and Gari?" Agusi soup is made from the dried seeds of a type of squash or gourd. Gari is made from ground cassava roots. I had eaten both on the boat when our Nigerian crew had prepared some for us. The men got excited, "Oh boy, you like Agusi?" When you eat that?" "We like it. Our crew made it for us—can you all make that?" I answered. They nodded and went on with their work. Even though we were trying to connect with them so they would look at us as people,

human beings like them, instead of just their victims, the night still ended the same as the night before, listening to them talk about killing us and about how they would spend the money they got for us. That's when we realized they were planning to do both. They planned to collect the ransom from our company and then murder the people who delivered it and us, making sure our bodies would never be found.

November 22nd—Day 5:

We woke up early again, ate some bread, and drank water. The men bringing us our food grumbled that Capo had not heard anything from our office and that the cell phone was still not getting a signal. We overheard the others talking again about going down the river to get a cell signal so they could call the company back and get an answer from them about the ransom. We sat in our hut and discussed what we would say on the phone to our supervisor if they were able to contact them. It's hard to know what words are important to say when you only have a short amount of time to talk, and it may be the last time you are able to speak to them.

Around noon, by our estimate, since the sun was straight overhead in the sky, the decision was made. The men approached the three of us and pointed, "Get in the bottom of the boat and lay down. Make sure you can't be seen. Keep your heads down." We backed out of our lean-to, and four of the men walked us over to the small ponga boat at the entrance of the mangrove. They kept their AK-47 rifles pointed at the back of our heads, prodding us if we slowed down. We got into the bottom of the boat as the rest of the men began chanting a prayer with their war beads for protection and favor. They partly covered us with a tarp but left plenty of breathing space. We ran down the river in the ponga for miles.

Once they stopped the boat, they had us all three stand and gave Tim the cell phone. They also had my handheld SAT phone that they had taken from my backpack on the boat. They handed it to Captain Tim, too. Tim used the SAT phone because it was able to pick up a stronger signal, and he phoned the office using the contact I had saved. The office picked up almost immediately. Tim asked, "What's the hold up on our release? People are getting impatient. We are running low on food, water, and medicine." We could all hear them answer on the speaker, "We've been trying to call but haven't been able to get through on the phone. It just goes straight to voicemail or no service." Tim replied, "Use this number for the SAT

phone. Do not call the cell phone number that they used before. There is a better signal on this phone. Did you get the number so you can call us going forward on this phone?"

CAPO grabbed the phone from Tim's hand, "If you don't pay, we will start hurting your men! So far, I haven't let my men harm them, but we will cut them if you don't bring the money. If you still don't pay, we will kill one of them so you will know we are serious—we will kill them, and you will never find their bodies!" Our office manager interjected quickly, "No—we will get you what you want. We haven't been stalling—we haven't been able to get you on the phone! We need to talk to each of the men, not just Tim. We have to know that they are all okay. We will not pay for any men that are hurt, and we won't give you money for three men if there are only one or two." CAPO handed me the phone, and I heard our coordinator's voice on the other end of the line. I asked, "Have you all talked with my wife and boys? Do they know what's happening?" He reassured me, "Yes, we've talked to your wife—your family knows what is happening. Is there anything you want them to know? Anything you want me to tell them?"

My voice trembled, "Please tell my wife and boys that I love them, that I am in God's hands, and that I will see them again soon, either at home or in heaven. Tell her not to worry because Jesus is with me." Capo took the phone from me and handed it to Antonio. "Tell my family I am okay for now and love them." Tim also told him to tell his wife and daughter that he loved them, wasn't hurt, and was all right for now. Capo took the phone from Tim and said gruffly, "You have until tomorrow to make a decision, and if it is the wrong choice, then we will take the extreme measures I spoke of." Capo cut off the call after he spoke and told the men they would wait for the sun to go down before taking us back to the little island where they had been holding us. "It will be safer if we travel with them after dark so no one can see them or identify us clearly.

While we waited, Sonny came over to me—"Tell me about this, Jesus. You keep praying to God to save you and telling us you don't want to die, but then you tell us you are in God's hands." I said, "Yes, my fate is in God's hands. If he wants me home with Him, then He will take me. If it is not my time to go, He will not allow you or your men to kill me, period. I really want to see my wife and boys again, so I pray to survive and go home to them, but if that is not what God has for me, then it is not, and more than anything, I want His will for my life and death. Sonny didn't

know what to think when I answered him like that, "I don't understand you whitey—you should be begging us for your life."

Soon after dark, we headed back to the camp, running down the river in the dark. The men made us lie down in the bottom of the boat again but didn't bother covering us. They just kept the tarp ready in case they met anyone on the river. When we got back to the camp, we saw some of the vines and tree branches had been cleared. Capo tested the SAT phone in different areas to see if he could get a better signal. The phone seemed to have more reception in the areas they had cleared. We got out of the boat and trudged wearily to our little hut. Talking it over, we didn't hold out much hope for a rescue. None of us could think of how our company would get the ransom of 1.5 million US dollars out to our kidnappers in the middle of the Niger Delta. We felt helpless. All we could do was hope for a better day tomorrow. Our kidnappers decided to celebrate that evening with lots of drugs and alcohol, their nightly ritual.

November 23rd—Day 6:

I woke up and saw the filthy hut and the mosquito netting, and despair crept into my heart. I prayed for God to fill me with the Holy Spirit—our Comforter. Each day was blending into the next. I started marking in the dirt with a stick to note the number of days we had been in captivity, including the day we were taken. Then I remembered we had spoken with the office yesterday, and the anticipation of our possible release grew inside me. We did not eat that morning. We just listened quietly to the men who had been partying all night. They were really out of it, and we could hear them again, "Let's just kill them! This is taking too long. We can take a loss on this one and hit another one of their boats. Then they will know we mean business. They will take us serious if they see we will do what we say, and they lose their men."

The men began naming different company boats that were possibilities for hijacking and kidnapping. They listed them to see which one they could agree on as the perfect hit. It was psychologically tormenting to be continually reminded of the different ways they could hurt or murder us. The leaders in charge were of a different mindset, but they weren't always around. At those times, I didn't know if the other militants would follow their leaders' plans for us or just kill us and be done.

CHAPTER 6

Around noon, one of the men brought us some food. They had cooked Gari and Agusi soup for lunch because they remembered Tim, and I liked it. Even though they just brought us a small amount, I took it as a hopeful sign that they were still trying to keep us healthy. Tim and I ate, but Antonio was sick to his stomach and couldn't eat anything. Over the sounds of partying and talking, we heard the SAT phone ring. Our hopes went through the sky! They didn't stay there for long, though. The news wasn't good. They were having a difficult time agreeing on a meeting point.

Capo called Tim over, "You—Tim—tell them Antonio is sick, very sick. Say he probably has malaria, and we are not going to get him any medical attention. Tell them he will die if they don't meet with us soon and give us the money. Maybe even tomorrow, he could die." We could hear Tim on the phone as he repeated what Capo said. He had a gun pointed at him, so he couldn't add any other words or answer any questions. That phone call really sent the men into a rage. Half of them went and grabbed their assault rifles. "Let's end this nonsense! Capo—we kill them, and then we go after another vessel. Then they know we mean business and will pay us even more!" Sonny strutted over and grabbed Antonio. "This one first—he is sick anyway!" Capo stopped him, "No! You all will do as I say. I am in charge here, and we will do this my way, the right way!"

Several hours went by before the phone rang again. Capo answered and put it on speakerphone, so all the men could hear what was said. "We have found a boat and have someone willing to come meet with you. He will bring the money to exchange for our men, all three men. They must be healthy and unharmed, or there will be no deal." Then, they began negotiating a time and place to meet. The company named a location to do the trade and a time that they could have the money to hand over to our captors. The pirates disagreed with their terms, changing both the place and time for the meeting, "If you don't have your man there for the exchange at the right time, or if there is any funny business, anything not by our terms—a change in the amount of money or people, we will kill Captain Tim first." Then he hung up the phone.

The men began shouting and jumping with the excitement of getting the money and finally being allowed to go home. They started partying again, celebrating this time. We returned to our hut and sat there under the tarp, whispering. "Finally, we get to go home!" Antonio said. "Can it be this easy? This is great!" I said quietly. Tim whispered back, "No, it can't be this simple. Something is not right. Who could they have got to

do the exchange? How did they get the money here? They haven't had enough time to set something like this up." The night went really slowly. We couldn't sleep. We had too much to think about; everything was happening to get us home, or so we thought.

November 24th—Day 7:

Seven days—an entire week since we were taken—kidnapped from the high seas. Today, we learned the true meaning of piracy! Today was the day that our company and MEND, Movement for the Emancipation of the Niger Delta, a militant group that had kidnapped us, had set up to exchange the ransom demanded for our lives and our release from captivity.

We woke up to no food again, and tensions were high. We were excited but stressed, and our captors had, for once, stopped drinking early the night before so they could get a good night's rest and be ready for action. They did not trust our company and were worried that the promised exchange could be some kind of setup to rescue us without turning over the money. They were also nervous about getting caught, imprisoned, or killed for their actions. We watched them warily from behind our mosquito netting. They were preparing for a war. We realized that this could go very badly for all of us. We could see them as they gathered together in small groups, praying to Jesus on the one hand to deliver a victory and then, on the other hand, to voodoo and praying for power to win over their enemies. We—our company and us—were the enemy. They began dressing in their battle gear, consisting of only war beads and pants. Standing shirtless in the clearing, each man entered into the rituals needed for battle and a wild dance around the burning fire pit. As we sat in our hut, I knew all three of us were wondering if we would live through the day. I began praying to God to please get us through this, to bring us home so I could be a husband to my wife and a father to our two boys. As I continued praying, I turned my desires over to God and asked that His will be done over what I wanted. If it was my time to go home to heaven, and that was His will, then that was my desire. I looked forward to meeting Jesus and was ready to do that whenever God wanted me.

The pirates packed up all of the belongings they had taken from our vessel and loaded everything into the two little ponga boats they had been using. They planned to put the three of us in one ponga with Capo and two of their men. Sonny and two others would travel in the other boat

to meet with the representative of our company and verify that they had the money. They wanted to physically see it and count it. The ponga boat we were in would be hidden a short way behind so they could take us out after they were assured of the ransom payment. At least, that is what was planned. As they were loading us on the small boat, we overheard them talking. Our kidnappers were the ones planning a setup! They were so worried that our company had arranged for their capture that they decided to make alternative plans. They would be ready as they neared the meeting place, and at Sonny's signal, the militants were to jump onto the ransom holder's boat and attack!

"We will kill all the occupants and take all the money." We heard Sonny say. Capo replied, "I will call from the SAT phone and say that the people never showed up. I will tell them they picked the wrong people to bring the money to us and that they must have stolen the ransom for themselves. No one will ever find their bodies or the boat. We will make sure of that!" He laughed. Tim, Antonio, and I looked at each other with despair. This was what we had been worried about. We knew you couldn't trust this MEND group, and over the past week, they had talked about how they could get the money for us without releasing us. We knew that if they killed the company's men and took the money, they would murder us, too. They had already talked about how they could cut our bodies up and feed us to the gators in the river.

As we pulled out from the riverbank, my mind raced over possible scenarios involving what we had overheard from our captors. I prayed, "Lord, don't let them hurt us or harm the people sent to rescue us." I didn't know who would be coming with the ransom, but I knew they were walking into a trap. The two boats glided to a stop at the entrance to the mangroves, and the men connected them together with a raft. The militants said a prayer and then muttered voodoo incantations. One of them reached into his pockets and pulled out some seeds, and they began chanting over them.

Another man laughed, "You can pray if you want." I was praying to God to please comfort our families if this went bad and keep us in His hands. The same man who took the seeds from his pocket handed some of them to us and told us to take them. "No way, we don't even know what it is," Tim said. The man answered, "It is voodoo; take it, or we kill you now!" They cocked their AK-47 rifles and pointed them at each of our heads. "Take it or die!" We unwillingly took the seeds, not knowing if we were poisoning or drugging ourselves, but not wanting to risk dying so

close to our release. Each of them took a big swig of gin and then sprayed the alcohol through their teeth all over each other. I guess it was one of their rituals for victory.

We left the mangrove area, and the two boats glided down the river. The men in our ponga said to lie down in the bottom and covered us with the tarp. It was a long way to the meeting place, and they didn't want anyone to spot us. I don't know how anyone who saw them wouldn't have been able to tell that something strange was going on. They were painted up, dressed for battle, and carrying guns. We were stressed about what could happen at the exchange, but we were also full of hope that we might be going home. When we finally got to the area they were looking for, we could feel the boats slowing down, and they turned right into a narrow river.

They took our ponga and continued a little ways farther down the river. They stopped and talked briefly, and then Sonny and his crew continued on farther to meet the company representatives. They had brought extra guns and ammo. The men we were with took us up the river, tucked the boat into a small tributary, and took off the tarp. We hadn't been there long when a family came by in a ponga and saw the three of us. They glanced at us and then looked away quickly. Capo took us up a little farther out of sight after that so no one else could see us. Since the word was out that a group of Nigerians had attacked an American oil supply boat and taken three hostages, the men were nervous about other people seeing us and taking us for themselves.

We sat there waiting for what seemed like forever. Capo looked at us and said, "Listen, guys, this is not personal, this is business, this is just business." I guess he was trying to convince himself that what he was doing wasn't wrong and that any suffering he caused was not on purpose. We just kept thinking about what was happening. Had Sonny and the other men snuck up on the men who had come to pay the ransom? Had they killed them and taken the money? Would they be returning only to kill us now? I prayed over and over—God, please don't let our captors kill these people; don't let them die because of us. The wait continued, so Tim, Antonio, and I started talking about what we wanted to do when we got home. Capo heard us talking about our children, and he told us he was doing this because he needed the money to send his kids to school. His wife also required surgery. The Nigerian Navy didn't pay very well, and the money our company paid his superior for protecting their supply boats stayed with the bosses and

never got passed on to the men providing the protection. He had planned this hijacking and kidnapping to get the money he needed.

Since Capo had started talking to us about our abduction and why he had been its organizer, I decided to ask him something we had been wondering about. "Why our boat? What made you choose our supply vessel? How did you all even know where we were? Our company pays you all to leave the orange and cream-colored boats alone." Capo looked at us and answered, "Yes, we have heard about the money paid to leave the boats alone, but since we never got any of that money—well, you see how it is." He explained, "A couple of years ago, the Nigerian government signed a treaty with MEND and other militant groups harassing the oil companies. They gave us amnesty for anything we had done in the past if we turned in our weapons. They also promised us money, training, and jobs. Most of us took maritime training. We are all trained as ABs or QMEDs [Qualified Members of the Engine Department—like oilers, electricians, and firemen], and we have STCW [Standards of Training Certification and Watchkeeping]. We were ready to work. We wanted to work, but no one put us to work. My men are hungry, and they need money for their families to survive." Tim replied, "But that doesn't tell us how you picked us; you even knew our names and exact location." Capo said, "I know a man—a Nigerian, that works on AGBAMI FPSO." Suddenly, it all made sense. The men working at AGBAMI FPSO (Floating, Production, Storage, and Offloading) knew each crew, what we were carrying, and our location at all times.

It seemed like we had been waiting for hours. Capo was getting more restless and wondering aloud where his team was. Not long after that, we heard the call they had agreed upon for their signal, "MoMoMow! MoMoMow!" Capo guided our ponga out of the small tributary we were hidden in and met the boat holding Sonny and his crew in the broader part of the cove. Sonny was agitated and more than a little upset. Capo asked, "What happened? You all were gone a long time. I was getting worried." I wondered if he had gotten worried about the exchange or that they had killed the people and run off with the ransom money, leaving him out of the loop.

They guided the two boats close together and moved out of sight. Sonny crossed over to our ponga and told Capo what had happened, "We met a group of men with a big bag. They were there waiting. We demanded to see the money, but it seemed like they knew that we were planning to kill them and take the money because the main chief told us before you do anything to us, let's talk. Then they handed us the bag. We opened it

up. It was full of food, water, and supplies. They could see we were upset, so the chief told us to wait, that they had brought some money too. They only gave us $25,000 US dollars in cash. As they gave us the money, more boats that were part of their team showed up. The chief said the money was to pay for supplies to care for their men—to feed them and keep them healthy, while they worked on getting the $1.5 million. He also told us there was no way they would have brought all the money because they knew we planned to kill them and steal the ransom. Someone with us is giving them information! Someone must have told them what we planned to do!" Sonny continued angrily, "They said they would call on the SAT phone soon to set up a safe place to exchange the hostages for the money but that we had better not try to pull any tricks on them."

We could see that Sonny was really pissed off. He and the other men from his boat started yelling at us. We couldn't understand what they were saying, but we knew they were enraged. They blamed us for what had happened, although they had to realize there was no way we could have had anything to do with the men knowing their plans to kill them and take off with the ransom money. Capo said, "I know you all are angry. This is going to take longer than we thought. I know you all want to go home. We all want to go home."

Sonny became infuriated. He grabbed his AK-47, "You whites—you get up!" The other men on the boat pulled us up and turned us around, so we stood there trembling with our backs toward Sonny. I was praying the entire time, God, your will be done. I couldn't remember the whole prayer, but I was saying the verse from the Bible, "No weapon that is formed against you shall succeed" (Isaiah 54:17a LSB). I prayed please, Lord, accept me into heaven. I repeated, "Though I walk through the valley of the shadow of death, I will fear no evil" (Psalm 23:4a KJV). I knew I wasn't making sense to those around me, but it didn't matter. I was talking to God, not them. I yelled, "No, No, NO!" as Sonny stood behind me and placed his gun against the back of my head. I could feel the cold steel of the barrel against my skull, and I knew he was going to pull the trigger. Sonny yelled, "Screw this, I am going home!" He cocked the gun, and I heard the sound as he pulled the trigger. Everything went completely black. Tears were streaming from my eyes. I realized I was still breathing—the gun had misfired! Capo jumped up and wrested Sonny's gun out of his hands. He pushed Sonny onto the other boat and said, "Not today. We are not going

CHAPTER 6

to kill these men yet." Sonny stood there in shock. He couldn't believe that I was not lying there with a bullet through my head.

To this day, I thank Jesus for putting his hand between the bullet and the hammer. There is no reason that gun misfired at that exact moment other than God's intervention. He kept me safe. God saved me from that bullet. After Sonny tried to shoot me in the head and Capo regained control of the situation, it took a while for the remaining men to calm down. They discussed their options and argued over what plan they would follow. They all decided they needed to start showing up at home, a couple of them at a time. They also agreed on a different place to hide us.

Capo decided that they should set up a camp in the area we were in for the night. They believed running back down the river in the dark wouldn't be safe because we would be traveling past several villages. Each of them had guards that could force them to stop and explain why they were there. The villagers would see they had three white men, and it would be over for them. All of their work and risk in taking us would go down the drain. Capo said, "We will start fresh tomorrow." Everyone agreed. Sonny had quieted down. He couldn't understand how I was still alive. His gun should have fired. I saw him checking it and talking to himself about what could have gone wrong. I knew—God had worked a miracle and saved my life.

The men began working to secure both boats to a tree so we could camp out for the night. Tim, Antonio, and I whispered to each other as best we could while they were tying up the boats. We were worried that the rest of the men would slit our throats and float us down the river as soon as Capo went to sleep. We had heard them discussing that as one of the things they could do to us. They had gone into great detail—even to say that afterward, they would go home for five days and then meet back up to return with the other ponga boat.

Capo refused to sleep the entire night while we were camping in the trees in the boats. He stood guard over us the whole time so none of the men would have a chance to follow through with their plans to slit our throats. None of us slept at all. I was numb, reliving the fact that an assault rifle had been placed against the back of my head, fully loaded. Sonny had chambered a round and pulled the trigger. I just kept repeating, "Thank You, God, Thank You, God," over and over. Capo told the men that they had to see this whole thing through no matter how long it took—that it would be worth it once they had the money. They finally all agreed with him. That relieved us, knowing they still thought we were worth keeping alive.

November 25th—Day 8:

We watched the sunrise that morning and felt a new hope. Early in the morning, the men made us lay down in the bottom of the ponga and covered us up so we knew they were taking us back on the main river. They took off their war beads and dressed in work clothes so they would not arouse any suspicion in the villages along the river where we were traveling. We set out, glad that we were in the ponga with Capo. We felt safer with him. We traveled up the river for about six hours or so to reach the new site they had decided to move us to. The boat turned into a cutoff in the river, and we were allowed to get up off the floor and take off the cover. We had slowed down a lot, and the land we were going through had more vegetation. It looked like we had gone inland, as the trees were different, too. Coming around a big bend, we saw a camp with a dock.

The other boat traveling with us was already there, and the men on it had gotten off and were standing waiting for us. They caught the lines when we pulled up and tied the ponga to the dock. When I looked toward the camp, I saw a little grass hut made entirely out of palm fronds. Once the boat was secured, Capo said, "Welcome to 'New York City'—your new home for as long as it takes your company to come up with the entire ransom money." We gathered our life jackets and got up onto the dock. He walked us to the grass hut and said, "This is where the three of you will be staying." We went in and saw a makeshift bed with foam on it. The foam they had brought from the first location was wet, so we left it outside the hut to dry in the sun. "Get busy and put up this mosquito netting around the area you want to sleep in here," Capo ordered. "Make yourselves comfortable. You will be here for the long run."

One of the men showed us the area to use as a bathroom. "Where is a good place for us to bathe? To clean ourselves?" I asked him. He took us down to another area and showed us the bucket to fill with water to rinse ourselves. The men had unloaded the big duffel bag full of supplies our people had given them. They gave it to us. It felt like Christmas opening that bag! We took out a sheet and placed it on the makeshift bed. The bed was larger than what we had been sleeping on. At least now we could lie on our backs to sleep and have more space. The place we were given to stay in was roomier than our last quarters, and there was an area where we could prepare food for ourselves. We pulled ramen and other nonperishable food items from the duffel bag.

CHAPTER 6

The other boat went to town so the men could spend some of the money our company had given them to buy bottled water. Of course, they spent some of the money on themselves and women, so they didn't buy enough bottled water for the three of us. We had to ration it carefully because we knew we would get sick without that water. Capo berated the men, "Give me the money. I can't trust you all to even go buy bottled water. These men will get very sick if they drink as we do." They sullenly gave him the money, making excuses for the fact that they hadn't followed his orders and didn't buy enough water. We decided to look around the area to find something to sit on. Tim spotted some big tree logs in different locations. We wanted three places we could move to if needed—so we kept searching until we found three locations where we could sit, and we moved the tree logs to those areas.

The three of us sat around the fire to rest and figure out where they had brought us. The witch doctor approached me and asked, "Where do you live? What is your wife like? Is she pretty?" I just looked at him. I wasn't about to give him any information about where my family and I lived. I didn't even want him to know the state. "What will you do if you leave here alive—then you go home with your pretty wife and children. You hear a knock on the door. You get up off your soft chair, and you open the door, and hahaha—It's me!" he cackled. "Well," I began, "I would ask you to come into my house and offer you some food—maybe a sandwich because that is the right thing to do." "Sure," he said. I continued, "Then I would put a bullet between your eyes because I know the only reason you would be there is to hurt my family, and I will never let you harm my wife and my children." He looked at me with his wild eyes and started laughing again.

After that, one of the men said, "So you have guns. Do you all three have guns? Do you shoot?" We all answered, "Yes, we have guns to protect our homes." The man held his gun out to us and said, "Here—take my gun. Let's see if you know how to shoot. Shoot that coconut over there out of the tree." I said, "No way, I am not taking your gun. You will say that I stole it from you and tried to shoot you. Then you will kill me." That changed the subject, and they started discussing their plan to hold us hostage in this new location. They let four of the seven pirates go home for a few days. When those guys got to town, they were supposed to get three of their guys, who were waiting, to come back down to help fortify the camp. Capo, Sonny, and one of their men stayed with us.

I was glad to see that the witch doctor left with the others. It would have been great if Sonny had gone, too, since he had tried to shoot me in the head, but at least Capo stayed at the camp to make sure they didn't kill us. After the men left, we cooked five Indome (ramen) bags for dinner. We shared it with the crew. Then I got a bar of soap and used the bucket to dip water from the river and rinse off. Oh my, what a great feeling it was to clean up! I also washed my coveralls, and I hung them up to dry. I didn't have other clothing, so I just walked around in my boxers. There is no modesty in the jungle. It was cooler here at this camp and windier, so we kept the fire going in our hut.

After relaxing briefly, we went through Tim's medicine bag and pulled everything out to check how many doses we had. We were getting low on the doxycycline hydrate, our antimalarial medication. We found more in his bag, but it was expired. We estimated we had about enough medication to last a month for three people. He also had two bottles of melatonin, which gave us about ninety of those; we definitely needed them to help us sleep. We did not want to be in this situation for a month and were praying our people would figure out something to get us out of here. They needed to give these guys their money so we could go home. Sonny seemed to be in a better mood now that he would be going home for three or four days. That lifted our spirits because he told us, "I guess now I will not have to kill you all!" We were able to go to sleep early that night and slept better than we had in eight days. We needed rest, and we needed food. All three of us had lost a lot of weight already.

November 26th, Day 9:

We awoke to our first morning in "New York City", as Capo had named our new holding area. You could say it was a city compared to the river isle where they had been hiding us. We made a small portion of oatmeal from the packets our company had sent in the duffle bag. I used the bottled water the men had bought in town to make tea for our breakfast. We finally had a good night's sleep, and I felt better for it. Yesterday had been a nightmare. Actually, this whole experience had been a nightmare, one we couldn't wake up from. We looked through the supplies again and realized we were down to one toilet paper roll. Tim brought it up, "Hey Capo, we will need some more toilet paper. We have only one roll for all three of us guys." Capo looked at us, "You can join the Stone Age like us when it's

gone. You will have to use your hand and then wash it, so either be careful how much of that roll you use or do like we do." He waved his hand to emphasize that he was serious. It was settling in our minds that we would be here in this place for the long haul. We needed to get used to that fact and figure out how to occupy ourselves.

I had brought the cross necklace I had made out of rope at the other campsite and one cross I had made out of palm fronds from there. I kept it with me in my back pocket. I gathered some sticks and began making more crosses for our bed and to place around our hut. I wanted to promote the crosses and what they stood for: God and his son Jesus Christ. I knew without a shadow of a doubt that God was with me. He had saved my life for something bigger than this, and I knew I would see my family again someday. I had to give myself a talking to whenever my mind went to my family, "Stop thinking about Stephanie and the boys, Rich. You need to focus on God and Jesus. He will get you through this. The goal is to get through it alive and with a sound mind. When you think about your family, you start getting too desperate and let fear into your mind. That won't help anything, so shut those thoughts away in your heart; don't let them into your head. God has a plan for you. God stopped that bullet from going into your head and killing you for a reason."

The boat with the reinforcements was due to arrive back soon. The guys went down to the dock as they saw the ponga draw in. We could see only two guys in the boat instead of the three or four they had mentioned bringing in. They secured the boat and brought presents for Sonny. They carried up a massive bag of Indian hemp or marijuana. That was the last thing they brought up. They sat around, smoked pot most of the afternoon, and caught up with what was happening in the town. One of the men who had just come in that afternoon got up and jumped in the river. It was so hot—we could not get cooled down, so I said, "Hey Capo, is it okay if I swim there in the river too? It's just so hot." "Yeah, sure, just make sure you don't try to swim off anywhere." He answered and lifted his gun to prove his point.

Tim and Antonio decided to join me, and we walked down to the dock and jumped in. The water felt so good and cool. After swimming around for a while, we climbed and sat on the riverbank. While the heat dried our clothes, we watched these little fish. I don't know what kind they were, but they were swimming there in the river. When the fish reached the riverbank, they left the water and walked in the mud. There were some weird creatures

around there, that's for sure. Antonio never got in the water again after he saw that. He was not doing very well at all. I believe that Tim and I had both come to some sort of peace about the fact that it could be some time before this was over. Antonio, though, really struggled with the reality of our situation, and the pain of it was eating him alive from the inside out.

After our clothes dried, we went to the hut and made ramen for dinner. We ate early, and then "Dr. Tim" pulled out his medicine bag and gave us our meds: one antimalarial pill and one melatonin. After that, it was time for bed. It was good to go to bed, try to sleep, and forget about everything for a minute. At least here, we had more privacy, and we could talk freely to each other about whatever we wanted. Even in the evening, it felt like it was 115 degrees out. Luckily, we had taken the melatonin, and I drifted off to sleep pretty quickly.

November 27th—Day 10:

The morning started about the same as the other days. One of the new men from the town had been assigned to stay up and keep an eye on us as well as watch the camp all night. They discussed their plans in front of us. Capo was scheduled to leave for a day, and another group would return the following day to relieve the men left behind. Sonny stayed with us as the other three men left on the boat. Now, it was just Tim, Antonio, me, and Sonny at the camp. Sonny, of course, had his AK-47 and a machete. We were worried about what he might do to us since Capo had stopped him twice from hurting us, and Capo was gone. We got up and gave Sonny some of the Indomie packets, and he began cooking them. We were outside the hut, and Tim and I stood at the door, looking in at Sonny while he cooked.

Earlier that morning, before everyone else left, we heard them talking about our location. Tim, Antonio, and I began trying to figure out which area they said we were at, and we thought we knew what buoy they referred to. We decided we must be only about three to five miles from the Onne Port Turning Buoy. Tim told me quietly, "Hey, there is just one person with us here now, just Sonny. There is a boat here, too. We could jump him and escape." I said, "Yeah, Onne Port is only about four miles away. We could make it." We eyed Sonny while he was cooking the ramen. He looked up at us, and it was like he was thinking the same thing we were—these guys could take me out, grab my gun, and then escape in the ponga. He got up, walked out through the door, jumped over a little river carrying his AK-47, and disappeared from

our view to stash the rifle behind a tree. Tim and I moved away from the door and sat down on a couple of the stumps. I said, "It's a bad idea, Tim. What if we are wrong about our location and are farther than we think from any town or port we know." "Yes," Tim replied, "Worse people than these could grab us. Some of the villages back here still practice cannibalism, and people who don't care about getting money for us could take us and kill us." I answered him, "We need to let God handle this and get us out of this situation instead of trying to take it into our own hands and maybe get one or all of us killed." We went back in and ate after Sonny was done cooking. He calmed down when he realized we were not going to try anything. Not much more happened the rest of the day. We didn't have much to do besides trying to think of how our company would handle getting the money. We were in an impossible situation in an impossible place.

November 28th—Day 11:

The sound of a boat woke us up in the morning. We looked out of the hut down toward the dock and saw the ponga returning with four men in it. They secured the boat, and we watched as Sonny headed to meet them. They got out and began walking toward him. We could tell he was happy. He laughed and joked with the men, knowing he was going home for a day or two since Capo was coming back. We fixed some of the oatmeal packets from the duffel bag for breakfast and then hung around outside after we finished eating. We always tried to listen to the men's conversations, hoping they might let some information drop about what was happening and if they had heard anything from our company.

A couple of hours later, we heard the sound of a boat motor and saw Capo coming up the river in another ponga. He docked and walked up to the hut to see how we were. Sonny took him aside to talk, but we could overhear them, "Hey, Capo—when you left that first night—I thought they were going to cause problems. I knew they were thinking about getting away from me, maybe even trying to kill me. They knew I was the only one here—I could see in their eyes that they were wondering if they should try to knock me out—all three of them take me down and escape. You know though, Capo, they didn't even try—they just helped me cook." We could tell that Capo was impressed that we stayed and didn't try to hurt or kill Sonny to get away.

About an hour later, Sonny and two of the new guys left. Now there were the three of us and three of them. We hung out and tried to stay out of their way. Two of the guys were just young kids. They wanted to be part of MEND and join the hijackers as part of their gang. We could hear them telling Capo they would do whatever he wanted them to if they could join. They went so far as to say they would kill Tim, Antonio, and me without hesitation. All Capo had to do was say the word. It sure wasn't comfortable to hear people offering to kill you just to prove their loyalty.

We sat around the fire for a bit, then went into the hut and looked over our food supplies. We could see we were getting low and would need to ration our food, so we agreed to eat only one small meal a day. We didn't want to ask our captors for food, thinking they might get tired of taking care of us and decide to get rid of us. We took our medicine and went to bed, hoping the next day would bring good news. That night, I dreamed of home again. I was there at the beach with the boys and my wife. I could almost feel the breeze and smell the salt air. Then I woke up and was back in the hut in the middle of the hot night. I just wanted to go back to sleep and escape our situation, if only in my dreams.

November 29th—Day 12:

Each day is melting into each other. Wake up, eat breakfast, and sit in the heat and think. What do you do when you are trapped on a small island surrounded by marsh and water and jungle on every side? You think a lot—look back over your life, and you pray a lot. Looking back at my past, I could see so many times that God protected me and kept me from harm. People used to joke when I was growing up that I must have two guardian angels, and they were working overtime to keep me alive. I was a risk taker and began partying in my preteens. I was given alcohol as a toddler to calm me down and sedate me because my grandparents, who took care of me, had trouble dealing with an overactive two-year-old.

My brother, Jeff, and I grew up in Winter Park, Colorado. I loved skiing and was good at it. I was on track for the Junior Olympics, and the area we lived in provided me with those opportunities. We spent all of our free time in the mountains. School was fine, but home was not. My mother left Brian more than once. The last time, she didn't come back. One day, I found my birth certificate and saw another man's name listed as my father. That was a shock! I had always believed Brian was my dad, and I never knew my mother

CHAPTER 6

had been married before and that her first husband was my biological father. I lost faith and trust in my parents and felt like I had nobody.

Brian had to travel a lot for work, and it was hard for him to leave Jeff and me alone when he was gone, so he got a job he didn't have to travel for in Salt Lake City, Utah. That way, he could be at home with us. We resented moving from the only home, school, and friends we had known. Salt Lake City was near the mountains for skiing, but not like Winter Park was, and combined with becoming a teenager, losing my friends, and leaving behind daily skiing, my favorite activity that took up most of my time, plus having learned the truth about my parenthood, I started down a destructive path. I began running around with friends who drank and smoked pot. I was rebellious and acted out in school. Looking back, I can see Brian had his hands full with Jeff and me and was doing the best he could to raise two boys by himself, but at the time, I resented him for taking me away from the life I had known and the friends that I had spent my whole childhood with.

During this time, my mother contacted Brian and spoke to him, asking if Jeff and I could visit her in South Padre Island, Texas. She lived there with Ken and thought it would be good for us to meet him and stay with them for a month. Brian wasn't too happy about the idea, but he didn't want to keep us from seeing our mother, so he flew us to Texas for the summer after school was out. Ken and Mom picked us up from the airport, and she cried, saying she had missed us so much and was sorry, but she had to leave to get her life straightened out.

I instantly felt a connection with Ken. He treated me like an adult. I liked him and felt comfortable around him. We had a great time that summer and had much more freedom to do whatever we wanted than in Salt Lake City. I spent the days at the beach surfing and drinking. Ken had a sailboat, and I helped out on that, too. Jeff and I didn't really want to go back to Utah. We were enjoying our lifestyle on the island too much, but we flew back to Salt Lake at the end of the summer. When we got there, we found out that Brian had moved to a larger house and had a serious girlfriend with three children. I was upset that, once again, no one had told me anything about moving and the change in our lives with a new family moving in. Jeff and I told Brian that we wanted to live with our mom. I know it hurt him a lot, but I didn't care at the time. I just wanted that free and easy, partying lifestyle that the island offered, and I thought living there would give me the independence I wanted.

Mom and I started butting heads pretty soon after we moved in. She enrolled us in the nearest school, and I quickly learned I didn't fit in. I had played football in Salt Lake City, and I decided to try to play here, too, but with the fights I got into and my grades going down, that didn't work out. All I wanted to do was hang out at the beach and surf. Jeff started Middle School. He was really into skateboarding. He and Mom got along a lot better than she and I did. Maybe I was just more rebellious. Things got pretty bad at home, and Ken asked me if I wanted to take some time away with him on his sailboat. What seventeen-year-old wouldn't want to ditch school and an unhappy home life and sail away from his problems? We took off with Jim's yellow Lab, Scupper, and sailed all over. We went to the Florida Keys and the Bahamas, sailing in and out of ports for groceries and docking wherever we wanted to visit. Mom brought Jeff to come visit for a couple of weeks in Florida.

I spent about six months sailing with Ken, and then I decided to try going back to school. I flew to Salt Lake City and returned to school, but I had already been away and living a carefree life without rules. Living with my dad now with his requirements and all the regulations to follow at school pushed me into rebelling. I wanted to be my own man, so I returned to South Padre Island and got a job. I moved in with a friend who was looking for a roommate to share expenses, and I got a job at a restaurant bar on the bay. The money was good with the tips, and I had a serious girlfriend. I was on my own, living the life I thought I wanted, regardless of anyone else. Yes, most of my life, I had pretty much gone my own way, alienating anyone who tried to tell me what to do, but after turning over my life to God and recovering from my addictions, I felt like I had started a new chapter in life.

November 30th—Day 13:

I woke up with a sense of peace. I dreamed I was home with my family, and the boys were shooting baskets while my wife and I weeded the flowerbed in the front yard. When I opened my eyes, I saw the palm frond roof and the walls of the hut, and that horrible feeling of being trapped enveloped me. I knew that Tim, Antonio, and I would spend another day waiting and wondering if the phone call would come to set up the meeting for our release or if it would be another day, week, or month. Routine had set in—wake up, get up, sit around, and eat our one meal a day, which was not even a bowlful of food. We tried to stay out of the way as much as possible to avoid getting

on our captors' nerves. It seemed like I prayed all the time in my mind and under my breath, "God, protect all three of us and take us home."

That afternoon, Sonny showed back up, which made me more tense since he had held a gun to my head and pulled the trigger, intending to kill me, but God had other plans. Two of the young men who were trying to prove themselves so they could join the group went back home. Now, we had a total of four kidnappers guarding us, including Sonny and Capo. The wait for the phone call was wearing on them also, and I could hear the tension in their voices. Nothing came that day, not even a call to check how we were doing. Just before bed, I was sitting outside and saw Capo over by a tree. I could hear him praying, "Jesus, please let them call, and the company bring the ransom for these men. Please don't make me have to take one of their lives to get this thing done." I can tell you that listening to someone pray sincerely to God, asking that they won't have to kill you, really hits you hard. I told Tim and Antonio what I had overheard, and they also freaked out over it. I prayed again, "God, your will be done. Your protection and promise are all I need." We didn't have a very restful sleep that night.

December 1st—Day 14:

We awoke to the start of another typical day. It's strange how something can become normal so quickly, even though you have never experienced it before. It was sweltering hot, just as all the days here had been, and there was not a cloud in the sky. I prayed my morning prayers and asked God to answer Capo's prayer that he would not have to take any of our lives. We had nothing for breakfast since we were down to one meal a day. At around lunchtime, we made five packets of the indome (ramen noodles) and split a bottle of water. We sat outside, trying to catch any breeze we could, hoping to cool down even a little bit.

Our captors began discussing their next moves. They didn't seem to care if we heard or not. One of the men asked, "Hey, Capo, how long are we going to sit here and wait for this company to give us the money for these men? It's already been two weeks, and we still have to take care of them." I was anxious to hear Capo's answer. Capo looked at each of the men and said, "I have been praying, and we will wait for the money; as long as it takes, one month or one year, whatever it takes, we will make it work. Does everyone understand?" The men just nodded, but they didn't look too happy about it. I looked at Tim and Antonio and whispered

quietly so the others couldn't hear me, "Oh man, I don't know if I'm going to make it one more week. I am so hungry and thirsty and so hot." But I knew that I would make it as long as it took.

I kept reminding myself of stories from the Bible where people had to wait. I knew if it took a week, a month, or a year, however long, God would protect me and provide for me or take me to his kingdom. A sense of peace came over me, which I knew was from God. It was a struggle every day, though, to overcome my fear, and I turned it over to God each day. Several times throughout the day and night, when I woke, I would look to Jesus Christ and pray for His strength and acceptance whenever my thoughts would go to the situation we were in—the threats from our kidnappers and how my family must be feeling not knowing if I was alive, or dead, or being tortured.

By mid-afternoon, Capo was struggling to explain to his men why our people hadn't called. He said, "Let me check the phone," as he made a quick call. "No, the phone is working just fine." The sun was lowering in the afternoon sky, and we were so bored, hot, and worn down. We went to the stump near the entrance to the hut and had just sat down when we heard the SAT phone ring. Our hearts started jumping out of our chests as our hopes climbed. Sonny ran over to get Capo, and they answered the phone, putting it on speaker so all the men could hear. They knew we were only about fifteen feet away and would be able to hear everything that was said, also.

We heard a man on the other end of the line say, "Hello, Capo. I imagine Sonny is there with you?" Capo answered, "Hello, sir. My friend, how are you?" I could see total confusion on Capo and Sonny's faces. They hadn't expected a call from this man, whoever it was, on my SAT phone. The man on the other end began firmly, "Capo, Sonny, I will tell you this right now, my friends. MY three whites better be okay and unharmed. I have the money you requested. This happens today, period! I know where you are, and I know every man that is with you. In fact, my men are looking at you as we speak. No tricks! I have your money, and you will meet me tonight with my three white men. You can send Sonny to verify the money—the ransom you asked for in exchange for all three of my whites. You have fifteen minutes to discuss it with your little team of four, and call me back in fifteen minutes! Or else you know what will happen. You know what I can and will do to all of you!"

While we listened, we could see Capo's face. He grew pale in fear, and Sonny slumped down, turning his face to the ground. We looked at

each other, and I whispered quietly, "Oh no, this could be very bad." We got up silently and went into the hut, where we climbed under the netting on the bed. Then Capo raised his voice, and we could hear the fear in it as he spoke to his team. The younger men said, "Ha—bring it on!" Capo cut them off, "You don't understand who this man on the phone is. He is called R.C." They asked, "Well, who is he? Who is this R.C.?" Capo answered, "He is bad, very bad. Holy cow, Sonny, how do these white people, this company, have this guy? No, no, no, we are all dead." His crew looked at him in shock. Sonny wouldn't even look up. Capo continued, "Right now, MEND has another group here watching us. R.C.'s guys have eyes on us. We have to call him back, get these whites to the boat, and get the boat started. We have a long distance to travel. Let's go! Now!" They looked at him, and one of the men said, "It's gonna take a little time to get our stuff together." Capo shot back, "Don't worry about any of your things. You won't need them. We will be paid."

Within ten minutes, Sonny came into the hut. He ordered, "Whites, get up and get in the boats. Don't worry about any of this stuff here in this hut. This is over today. We are leaving, and you are either going home, or you are going to die—that's it." We didn't waste any time. The men loaded us into the boat and pulled away from the island. They had a bottle of gin mixed with some other liquid in their hands. They stopped the boat and prayed to their war god. Then, they banded red scarves and war colors on their bodies. They tried again to get us to eat the seeds. Again, we refused because we were afraid of what it was. They pointed their AK-47s at us and ordered, "Take or die."

Even Capo joined in, saying, "We will kill you if we need to because we are all dead anyway." We swallowed the seeds as they alternated between drinking shots of gin and spraying it all over us. They forced us down into the bottom of the boat again and covered us up like they had the last time. They had their gun barrels pointed right in our faces, which were show-ing through the side of the tarp. We were terrified. The boat bounced and jumped all over as it raced through the water. I was afraid the guns would go off when the boat leaped up in the air and slammed back down into the river, jostling their fingers they kept on the triggers.

I don't know how long it took to travel down the river, maybe two or three hours. I was knotted up from the tension, the hope that we would be going home, and the fear that the same thing would happen this time—or worse. The boat veered over to the side of the river suddenly, and Sonny

and one of the other men jumped out. The others still in the boat kept their guns pointed at us. I prayed to God that all was good and that we would see our families again if it were His will.

It was probably only ten minutes, but it seemed forever when we heard Capo's phone ring. It was Sonny calling. We could hear him through the line, "The money was there. We are one minute out, and we have to be down the river in five minutes. They got back in the boat, we took off down the river, and then they pulled up on a beach. The men rushed us out of the boat and hurried us up the beach past a hill onto a sandy road. We stopped there. We could see two men. They looked like sheiks coming down the road carrying a large duffle bag. They were both holding the bag; it was so heavy. As they approached us, they dropped the duffel bag and emptied its contents onto the ground in front of them.

One of the men asked, "Are you three okay? Have they harmed you physically in any way?" All three of us called out, "Yes, we're alright. They haven't hurt us!" The man told us to get behind them and began calling someone on the phone. Sonny was sitting on the ground counting the money and yelled, "There's not enough here—you all are short some of the money." He got up and came towards us, speaking angrily, "We will keep one of these men—either Captain Richard or Captain Tim until you bring us the rest of the money!" Capo looked at Sonny and ordered, "No, Sonny—put the money in the bag. We have to go." Then Capo looked at us and said, "Whites, this was just business—this is what we had to do for business, not against you." I looked at Capo and Sonny and said, "God wants me to forgive you, so know this: I forgive you for what you have done." They got into their boat, and just like that, they were gone. We could hear their boat motor as they went upriver.

We turned around and started walking up the sandy road. We still didn't know who had us or who had paid. It could have been someone besides our company. All we knew was that Capo had told his crew that it was a bad dude, R.C. I was walking quickly, wanting to get away from everything. Tim and Antonio said, "Captain Rich, get back here. We are surrounded. Walk slowly with us." Little lights started coming on, and red lasers streamed through the darkness. It seemed like hundreds of people were there. We saw someone, like a giant, next to an SUV at the end of the road. My heart was beating so fast. I was sure everyone could hear it.

As we approached, the big man beside the SUV called out, "Are you sure you are all okay?" I replied, "Yes, but they did a good job of making us

think they were going to kill us and eat our dead bodies." He said, "I want to apologize on behalf of the Nigerian people. They call me R.C." I am not exaggerating—this guy was huge. He stood at least 6'8" and looked to be solid muscle. His skin was covered in scars. I had heard his name before. He was a warlord, but I thought he was in prison for crimes committed in Sierra Leon. No wonder our captors had been afraid when he called on the phone. R.C. said, "I am here on behalf of Chief, a good friend to your bosses. I have come to get you out of here. But we aren't safe yet. We have to get through three roadblocks. You will say you work for Shell at their refinery here." We nodded at him, but I think we were all in shock that we were actually out of the hands of our kidnappers and just praying nothing stopped us or happened to us on the way out of the area.

We got through the roadblocks without much trouble. I had my cell phone that our kidnappers had given back to me when they realized I had no signal where they were keeping us. As soon as we got in range, I called my wife. I could hear the tears in her voice as she said, "Rich—Rich, is it really you?" in disbelief. "Yes, honey—I can't talk long now because the others need to call home too, but I just wanted to let you know that I am free, and I'm not hurt." She answered, "I love you so much, and I'm so grateful you are alive and safe." I said, "I love you—I have to go now, but I will call you back when we get to the safe house. I gave Tim the phone; he called his wife and then handed it off to Antonio so he could call home, too.

About forty-five minutes later, we arrived at the hotel where Chief was waiting for us. He greeted us, "My friends, I am so happy to see you." Then he turned and spoke to the man who rescued us, "Thank you so much, friend." R.C. answered, "I was happy to help my old friend. Is there anything else I can do to assist in this matter?" Chief smiled, "Yes, yes, you can. Track down Capo and Sonny and get the ransom money back. When you have them, call me for further instructions." R.C. nodded, "It will be as you say."

We followed Chief upstairs. He took us to our rooms and gave each of us a pair of shorts and a white T-shirt. He pointed to a door down the hall and said, "Go shower and clean the dirt off. Then you can get dressed and meet me there in my room. We will celebrate your release." It felt so good to take off the filthy clothes I had worn for the last two weeks and step into a shower. As the water poured down on me, I picked up the soap and tried to scrub off the grime that stained my skin. I didn't think I would ever feel clean again. After washing as much off as possible, I got out of the shower, dried off with the hotel towel, and put on the clothing Chief had given me.

I couldn't believe I was free. I walked down the hall and met Tim and Antonio in Chief's room. He had snacks and Dom Perignon champagne waiting for us. He said, "Welcome, my friends. Let us celebrate your freedom!" I asked for orange juice. I had made it this far—through all of this without touching alcohol, and I wasn't about to start now. After ordering some juice for me, he said, "Excuse me, I must call your manager and let him know I have you safe here. I am sure he will want to speak with each of you." We were on the phone with our manager in Louisiana for a long time. He wanted to get as much information on the men who had taken us and where we had been held as soon as possible while it was still fresh in our minds and they could start tracking them. Chief sent us to our rooms to get some rest after the three of us had given descriptions of our kidnappers and where we were held.

We had five hours at the hotel until our transport to Port Harcourt arrived. I got back in the shower and stood there for about an hour, letting the cool water rain down on my head and back. I was still so hot. After I got out of the shower, I ordered some food. I was starving, but I took one bite when it arrived and could not eat anymore. I called my wife and talked for a while but couldn't say much over the phone because the call could be monitored, and I didn't want to give away our location. The guys wanted to call their families again, so I gave them the phone and tried to lie down and rest for a little while. I was exhausted but couldn't sleep because I could not stop thinking about the last fourteen days. I thanked God over and over for getting us out of the situation and prayed that we would make it home.

Early the following morning, we met downstairs in the hotel lobby. Chief was waiting there for us. We saw a van pull up outside. Our base manager from Port Harcourt was sitting in it. Chief said his goodbyes because he wasn't traveling with us for the next part of our journey. We exchanged contact information with him. He smiled at us, saying, "You stay in touch. I will be in Louisiana in a month." We waved and thanked him as we got in the van. I was so happy to sit in the van and see someone I knew besides Tim and Antonio. Our manager was beyond happy to see us. I don't think I had ever seen him smile so much.

As the van pulled out of the hotel, a big army truck pulled in front of us, and another army truck pulled right behind us. They were troop trucks, and we could see they were loaded with men holding weapons. They were not taking any chances on our getting waylaid on the road by rebels. Our manager told us that we were five hours out of Port Harcourt.

CHAPTER 6

I looked at Tim and Antonio and said, "Wow, it's a good thing we didn't take off from 'New York City' when we were alone there with Sonny. We were nowhere near Onne Port like we thought. We would still be lost back there in the jungle or dead."

The troop trucks ensured that we made good time to Port Harcourt. They never slowed. It didn't matter if anything was ahead of us on the road; they just pushed the cars out of the way with their huge bumpers. Nothing stopped us. Our manager told us we were going to a camp with an International SOS clinic that provides medical services to make sure we hadn't picked up any infections or diseases that could prevent us from leaving the country.

When we arrived at the camp, they hurried us out of the vehicle straight into the SOS clinic. They took blood samples and ran the test results in-house to ensure we hadn't picked up any diseases or parasites we could bring into the United States. They sent us to clean up again, and our manager took us to his apartment, where he had our personal items salvaged from the boat. We showered again and shaved. I didn't think I would ever feel clean enough again. He ordered four pizzas for us since he knew we had to be starving. I could only eat one slice, even though I still felt hungry. I put one small suitcase together from my items found in the boat and gave the rest to my driver for his family. I didn't need it anymore since I knew I was going home and would never return and work here again.

We went back to the SOS clinic to get our results. The doctor at the clinic spoke with each of us separately. All of my test results came back negative. I didn't have any parasites or diseases. The bottled water and the antimalarial medication had done their job. The doctor also asked me about how I was feeling mentally and emotionally. I answered him honestly, "I don't know right now. I am exhausted, and I am so relieved to be going home. I feel like I'm in a daze." He told me, "When you get back to the United States, you need to get some help. You need to see someone—a psychologist or psychiatrist who has experience dealing with PTSD. I will contact your bosses with all of your medical results and rec-ommendations. You also need to see your family doctor and have some more in-depth tests run."

After our medical tests, they loaded us back into the van and drove us to the Port Harcourt Airport. We still had a military escort, and they walked us into the airport. Several people were working who recognized us from our flights to and from work. It seemed like they knew what had

happened to us. They kept saying they were so sorry and thanked us as we walked by. Our escort took us through security, and they didn't stop us to check any documents or luggage. They took us ahead of the people waiting to board the jet and loaded us first. I was glad our base manager was traveling with us because I don't know if any of us, Tim, Antonio, or I, could have handled getting ourselves onto the plane, much less deal with tickets, our luggage, or finding our seats. We had all flown many times, but we were physically, mentally, and emotionally exhausted.

We landed on a runway on the domestic side of the airport in Lagos, Nigeria. The airport has domestic and international flights, sharing the runways. When we debarked from our airplane, we could hear a bunch of commotion outside the doors in front of the luggage carousel. We picked up our bags, and they led us through the doors so we could head to customs to catch our international flight to the United States. As soon as we exited, officials surrounded us. They introduced themselves, "We are from the United States of America State Department. The gentlemen with us are with the FBI and CIA. We will be traveling with you on your flight to Atlanta. You need to come with us—we have a transport to take you to International Departures."

We didn't know which man was with what department, but they were all dressed in dark suits and looked very official. Our manager said, "Thank you, but we have arranged transportation with our company." We followed him to where our contact from Lagos was waiting with a company van. As our van left to take us to the International Departures side of the airport, we could see they had closed off a lane for us. Our manager drove us straight up to the front entranceway. We got out of the van, and another man in a suit opened the door to the airport for us. As we went in, he introduced himself, "Hello, I am the Director of the US State Department. You men don't need to worry anymore. It's all over." I looked at him and said, "You don't have a clue. The men that took us—The Capo in charge is a Nigerian Navy Captain, and his second in command, Sonny, is a Nigerian Army Sergeant. Who knows? Half of the Nigerian military men at the airport could have been involved. No—it's not over yet. It will be over when I am standing in the United States of America and not in the country of Nigeria. Then it will be over."

A Nigerian man in a suit walked up and said, "I am the head of security at the airport. I will take you through to get you checked in, and then I will walk you through the security checkpoint myself." As we approached

CHAPTER 6

the line for flight check-in and security, he said, "No, follow me." He walked us up to the front of the line and stopped the other passengers. He led me to the podium, where they checked my passport and flight information. I then went to the tables appointed for baggage inspection. I recognized one of the inspectors from past flights. He looked at me and said, "No, no need to inspect—you are good bros. We are sorry about what you went through here in our country." I went to the ticket counter, and they gave me my ticket. I looked at the man who had taken me through, "Wow—thanks, boss." I was right up front, which meant a better line to go through the security check.

I waited for Tim and Antonio to finish the inspection and ticketing. Once they joined me, an FBI agent, our manager, and the head of security led us to the first-class line for security. I told the FBI agent, "We always have problems with these guys at security. They are real pieces of work." We were next. One of the security checkers began yelling at us. You could tell he was furious. He was getting red in the face. The head of security stepped out from behind me. The man immediately changed his attitude, "Oh, hello, sir." Our escort didn't give him time to explain what he was yelling about. "Is that how you treat our guests! You are relieved of duty immediately. Go clean out your locker!" He snapped his fingers and handed our passports to another security officer. He told him, "Please stamp these passports for our guests. Then make sure your rude coworker leaves." He turned to us, "Sorry, gentlemen. Please follow me." We trailed behind him as he walked us through security and up to the lounge. He left us with our manager and the FBI agent to wait two-and-a-half hours until our flight arrived.

We sat discussing everything that had happened. After only an hour, we were alerted to go to our flight gate. Our manager and the agent walked with us down to Delta Gate. Several people were waiting at the gate. The head of security met us there. The gate agent looked at our tickets and passports and said, "Please follow me." We said goodbye to Antonio. He was taking a different flight since he was going home to his family in Mexico. Tim and I followed the agent, and he led us onto the airplane. Our manager, Tim, the FBI agent, and I were the only ones on the plane.

Our escorts left us after Tim and I were seated, so I have the feeling they were told to make sure we got on the plane and into our seats for departure. It wasn't very much later when they began boarding the remaining first-class passengers. Neither Tim nor I had been able to eat much or sleep since we were rescued. The flight attendant told us, "You gentlemen look like you

could use a rest." She must have laid my chair back because I don't remember doing it or anything else after she spoke to us. All I remember is opening my eyes and the attendant saying, "You need to put your seat up, sir, because we are landing." I looked at her and said, "I thought we were flying through to Atlanta. Isn't that a thirteen-hour flight?" "Yes, sir, you slept almost the entire way. We are preparing to land in Atlanta, Georgia." "Sorry, I haven't slept or eaten much in about two weeks." "Yes, sir, we were informed, and I woke you to eat dinner. After you ate, you went right back to sleep, though." I didn't even remember eating dinner. We got off the jet, and Tim said, "Let's go, bro. We should hurry to passport control to beat the people coming off our flight so we won't have to wait in a long line."

Another jet was debarking at the same time as ours. Standing in line, we heard an announcement over the loudspeaker, "Captain Tim Johnson and Captain Richard Tarpey, Captain Tim Johnson and Captain Richard Tarpey, please make yourselves visible." Both Tim and I raised our hands and waved so they could find us. FBI agents surrounded us and asked us to hand over our passports. One of the agents checked the passports and told us, "Come with me, please." The agents took us to the front of the line. Some passengers who had flown with us from Nigeria saw us and said, "Holy cow, what did you guys do?" As we approached the checkpoint counter, the FBI agents showed their credentials and told the men to stamp our passports. After our passports were stamped, we went and got our bags.

The agents took us out and led us into CBP—United States Customs and Border Protection. I looked at them and asked, "Why are you taking us in here? We have a flight to catch to New Orleans. Our families are waiting for us there." Two men stood behind the desk and said, "Alright, that was fast." The agent replied, "We need to clear these men in the National Data Base. These are the sailors who were kidnapped and held in the Nigerian jungle. I looked at Tim, and I got down on my hands and knees on the floor right there and kissed the ground. "Now it's over, buddy," I told him. One of the FBI agents looked at me and said, "We don't have any idea what you all have been through, do we?" "Nope, you don't," I answered.

We left the CBP office, and the agent said, "We will book new flights for you. You are not going anywhere until we have debriefed you. We are taking you both to our office." He continued, "We can do it here at our office, or we can take you to our office in downtown Atlanta." I looked at him incredulously, "I have a wife and two boys, and Tim here has a wife and a young daughter who are waiting for us in New Orleans. They have

been through a lot, and they just want to see us again." Tim spoke up, "Our families don't know anything about us except that we are alive, and they want to know if we are okay." The man said," Then let's get started." They separated us into different interrogation rooms.

The agent I went with took me into the room, sat me down, and began firing questions at me. He wanted to know why we had been targeted, how the hijackers had known who we were and where we would be, where they kept us, how they had treated us, if they had identified themselves, and why we had been released. After all the questioning, we met back together. They spoke with each other and then came back to us and said our stories checked-out. I asked, "Please get us to our flights then." The agent who had interrogated me answered, "Don't worry—we have taken care of that." We grabbed our bags, and they put us on an electric cart. Off we went to our flight's gate. They had ordered the plane to be held for forty minutes so we could make the flight.

When we pulled up to board the plane, the pilot was waiting for us at the gate. He opened the door, and we boarded, taking our seats. Everyone stared at us. We apologized for holding up the plane, but no one said anything. The flight attendant said, "Don't worry. The pilot announced over the intercom that we were waiting for two sailors who needed to get to New Orleans and see their families. Then the pilot approached us in our seats and said, "Welcome home captains." Once we landed in New Orleans and the door opened, the pilot announced over the intercom for everyone to have a great day. We looked around, but no one got up to leave. The flight attendant said, "They are waiting for you to go first." Oh man, I already had a lump in my throat.

Tim and I got up, grabbed our things, and debarked from the plane. As we began walking towards the exit into the waiting area, I could see Joe, one of the men I had spent some time with from my company, standing there with another man filming us. Then I looked past them and saw my wife and our boys. They were the best sight in the world! I couldn't believe it. Just a few days ago, I had not known if I would ever see my family again, and now here I was with them. They ran up to meet me as I walked towards them, and I wrapped my arms around all of them. I gave thanks to God that He had brought us back together again. Then I saw my sister-in-law and brother-in-law, Darla and Daniel, there too, and they came and joined us. I didn't want to ever leave the arms of my family again.

Chapter 7

As Rich finished going over the hijacking, their kidnapping, and release, I saw how God had truly blessed us and saved him and the other men from torture and death. It could have gone wrong at any time, during any part of their capture, captivity, or release. Looking at Rich, you could see the toll this had taken on him. Still, when he spoke, you could also see that God's spirit had kept him close, and instead of dwelling on the possibility of death, He had lifted Rich up and given him hope. Hope that no matter what, he would be okay. If he died, he would be in heaven with Christ; if he lived, he would be home with us. When Rich talked about the release, he mentioned over and over about forgiving the men who had kidnapped him and mentally tortured him. I could see how important it was to him and his life that he forgave them and did not harbor anger or hatred against them for everything that had happened. He had seen the desperation that they were fighting against for their people and that they felt it was justified to try to support their families and villages by taking from those who had so much.

Rich knows the damage unforgiveness, anger, and resentment can do. It can lead you down a path of addiction, and he knew deep inside that God had His arms around him and that what happened to him was under God's control. His freedom, that freedom from his past life and pain, came from Christ. Jesus says, "So if the Son sets you free, you will be free indeed" (John 8:36 NIV), and that freedom cannot be taken away. Paul writes, "For I am convinced that neither death nor life, neither angels nor demons, neither the present nor the future, nor any powers, neither height nor depth, nor anything else in all creation, will be able to separate us from the love

of God that is in Christ Jesus our Lord" (Romans 8:38-39 NIV). Rich has learned the truth in those verses.

I squeezed Rich's hand as we neared corporate headquarters and glanced at him, "I bet you are getting tired of telling everyone about it. You had to go through everything with the manager in Nigeria, the FBI in Atlanta, me, and now you have to repeat it again with corporate." "No, it helps to talk about it—I can't believe I'm really here with you after the last two weeks of thinking I would never see you or my family again." He reached across the car console and gripped my hand, squeezing it. I could feel the nervous energy radiating off him. I was worried the stress would trigger his addiction to alcohol and drugs. I had tried not to let my mind think about that—the chance that this trauma could send him spiraling down into the darkness of addiction again. I prayed that God would keep him from those desires and heal his pain and traumatic stress from what he had endured.

Rich looked at me and said, "Don't be upset, Stephanie, but I need to smoke a cigarette. I know I stopped smoking a long time ago, but I started again while they were holding us in the Delta. It helped my nerves and my shaking. I'm sorry, and I will quit again." I was so thankful that smoking was the only thing he had picked up again during his captivity. I replied, "I have been so scared and worried about you, honey. I imagined everything in my mind, and I had to just turn it off because I couldn't live with the thought that they were hurting or torturing you." He said, "I guess you were relieved hearing about what happened then, that they didn't torture us physically, just mentally." I rubbed his shoulder and answered, "Of course, I am so glad they didn't kill or torture you, but honey, the fact that they threatened you with machetes, shot off their guns, and tried to poison you with their moonshine mixed with drugs and that you were able to stand up to them and tell them that they might as well shoot you with their guns—that you wouldn't take a drink even if it killed you because that would be as good as signing your death warrant—that shows me how strong you had to be and I thank God that He was there with you holding you and protecting you." Rich said, "I know that God took me out of drug addiction and alcoholism, and He delivered me out of this alive."

I wanted to just be somewhere alone with my husband and hold him in my arms so he could rest and start to heal, but we were nearing the company corporate offices. These people had worked so hard to free my husband and their other employees. The sky was stormy gray, the wind was blowing, and rain started spitting on us as we pulled into the company

parking lot. The building was several stories high and much larger than I realized. I knew it was a big company, but since it was family-owned, I guess I just thought of it as a small-town "mom-and-pop" business. We got out of the car and walked over to where Tim and his family were waiting in the foyer so we could all go in together. As we crossed the open first floor, we saw people standing everywhere. All the employees had gathered and began clapping as Tim and Rich walked through the building and up the tall staircase. Rich held my hand as we climbed the steps, and he and Tim waved at everyone as we went through. People were crying and welcoming them with hugs as we passed their offices. Many of them approached us and told my husband and Tim that they had prayed daily for their safety and release. I was overwhelmed and grateful for the love and care that these people had felt for my husband and their prayers for his release.

We followed one of the human resources employees into a huge conference room. The owner of the company, his children, who were co-owners, and several others sat around the massive table. I saw the guy who had filmed us at the airport and whom Rich had spoken to as we got in the car to drive to the office. He smiled at Rich, came over, clasped his shoulder, and introduced himself to me as Joe. We shook hands, and Joe looked at the company's owner and said, "I have a good one for you. One of the first things this man here asked me after he got off the plane was if he would still have a job with our company because he was NEVER going back to Africa!" The owner replied smiling, "This is my company. I own it, and after me, my son will be in charge. You will have a job with this company for as long as you want and can work wherever you like."

A block of seats was set aside for Rich, me, Tim, and his wife. Antonio had flown straight home to Mexico, so I didn't get to meet him. Joe then began introducing us to everyone around the table. I had met some of them when they flew to our home to speak with me. I walked up to the company's owner and hugged him, thanking him for bringing my husband home. We were also introduced to the hostage negotiator that had been hired.

One of the men handling most of the information with the Nigerian office spoke to us about how the release had gone, "I know you all were kept in the dark about most of this. In fact, only a few people in this room knew about the plans to pay the ransom and set up the release. We knew that paying the ransom would be dangerous for whoever the drop-off person was because, in these countries, the kidnappers would take the ransom and kill the person who brought it. Then they can claim they never got the money

CHAPTER 7

and that no one had shown up to pay them. That way, they can get paid double or can try to get a ransom from the families, too. If no one else pays them, they get rid of the hostages and still get their money. The first release was set up for Thanksgiving Day. We had one of the local heads of a village working with us. We had contracted him to deliver the payoff money. It had been set up that he would go in by boat to an area the kidnappers had chosen and deliver the ransom money. They told him to come alone and unarmed. He agreed to go in, but he had a different plan. It was good that he did because the kidnappers didn't bring you all with them, and they tried to attack and kill him. He called out, and his men came out of the surrounding area with weapons. Chief gave the militants a bag of supplies for our men and some cash to buy bottled water and more food. He told them we would be in touch to set up the ransom exchange, and that he would be prepared to make sure sure they didn't double cross him. That's why we didn't tell you all anything about the exchange plans, because just one little thing goes wrong, and the whole thing is off, or the men are dead."

I sat there listening and remembered that on the day before Thanksgiving, one of the company's men had mentioned that it wouldn't be long until they would bring the men home. "When the kidnappers called back, they accused the Chief of trying to steal the money, and we had a serious discussion with them on the safety of the men and that we were not going to deal with people that were trying to pull something on us or on our delivery people. We asked them if they wanted the money or not—we had to play hardball with them so they wouldn't try to pull anything again like they had with Chief." Rich and Tim both related that they had overheard the men talking and that what Chief said was true. The kidnappers did try to kill him and grab the money.

The company representative continued, "We told them that all three men had to be in the boat with them for the money exchange and that we had to see and identify them to make sure they were the right people and that they were alive and well before the money was handed over. We also assured them that if they were armed, our men would carry weapons and that if they tried anything else on us—that was it—no money. We were not going to risk the lives of other people, so they had to be straight with us, and the money and the men had to be traded at the same time." The negotiator put in, "Our firm has handled many international hostage situations involving oil workers in Nigeria and other countries in Africa. Our main concern was that the kidnappers were just that—hijackers and kidnappers

out for money, not out to make a statement and execute some Americans. From all of our dealings with these kidnappers, their aim seemed to be financial. We have found that keeping the kidnappings out of the news and out of the hands of the media decreases the chance that something will go wrong and that the kidnappers will decide they want the publicity and notoriety instead of cash."

The company rep continued, "We set up a new meeting for the exchange and this time everything went smoothly. I think the hijackers were worried that they had the men too long and that someone would find out or another group would kidnap you all from them and then start a new ransom situation." Tim said, "We knew something was up because they had us get our stuff together and wait for the head guy to bring a boat in." Rich added, "They were excited and getting wild, boasting about what they would do with the money. They made us lay down in the boat and covered us with blankets. They got quiet when we started running through the channels and told us not to make a sound. We were exchanged when the money was handed over, and then they took off in case the kidnappers decided to start firing on them." I sat in the chair in the conference room, thinking how surreal this was. I felt like I was reading one of the adventure novels my husband liked and that he and I were a part of that. You never dream of these things happening to you or your family. You can't even imagine them as part of your life.

After we ate, Tim's wife and I were taken on a walking tour of the facilities and headquarters by one of the employees while Rich and Tim went to their debriefing. On the tour, I got to see what a big operation Rich's company ran, and I was introduced to many of the people I had spoken with through emails or on the phone. It was interesting, and my tour guide was very nice, but I was tired and didn't want to be apart from Rich. I had just gotten him back, and I wanted to look at him and soak in that he was really here and not a figment of my imagination. I was so relieved when Rich and Tim returned from the debriefing, joining us near the end of the tour. The insurance people with the company told us that the men would have to see a psychiatrist to be evaluated for PTSD and be cleared medically before returning to work. They also gave us phone numbers of some FBI agents in the Rio Grande Valley who might be able to recommend someone. I told them we would probably get a recommendation from our doctor because I wanted Rich to receive PTSD counseling from a Christian therapist. We had not had a good

CHAPTER 7

experience with a psychiatrist earlier in our lives who used chemical mind-altering medications to treat Rich for his addictions.

Rich and I met with the human resources department to set up the paid leave information they needed. The company's owner told Rich and Tim they could take as much time as required. They would be paid the same as if they were still at work on the ship. They told us to send all of Rich's medical expenses, including the PTSD counseling, to them. They would also pay for our travel. After completing all the paperwork needed, Rich and I said goodbye. We drove back into New Orleans to the hotel the company's agents had booked for us across the street from the airport. They had bought our tickets and offered to pay for our meals while we were in New Orleans.

We met Tim and his wife, checked into the hotel, and went to eat dinner with them in the hotel restaurant. I had no idea what we had for dinner; I was too preoccupied with getting my husband back. I could have eaten cardboard and not known it. We talked about our children, and Tim and Rich talked briefly about how they felt.

We were exhausted, and since we had early flights out the following day, we said goodbye and went to our hotel room. We called the boys and Daniel and Darla as soon as we got to our room. They were staying the night in Houston and would be home the next day to pick us up at the airport. Rich showered first, saying he wanted to rinse off all the smells from his airline flight home. By the time I got out of the shower, he was fast asleep. I knew he was emotionally, physically, and mentally exhausted. Today had been grueling—going over everything again and dealing with the interrogation at the Atlanta airport. I couldn't sleep very well. I just kept dreaming that Rich was still gone, and I woke up throughout the night to check that he was really there.

We got up in a rush the next day, dressed, and made it to the airport in time to have a quick breakfast of beignets and café au lait. I bought a package of beignet mix at the airport to make some for the boys. Rich's nerves were still shot, and mine weren't that great either. When you have been through something like this, you don't just bounce back to your usual self—I don't think you are ever that same person again. It changes you in ways you don't even know at first. We boarded the airplane, and our flight left as scheduled. My parents, Darla and Daniel, and the boys were waiting for us at the airport. On the drive home, I asked my husband if he had called his parents yet, but he said he would after we got to the house. He

was not ready to go over it all again with them. I had called them after I found out he had been rescued, but I know they were waiting to find out how he was, everything that had gone on, and to hear his voice.

When we got home, Rich sat on the back porch with the dogs, staring into the backyard and soaking everything in. We had so many people and churches praying for Rich's return, so I had my parents and my sister help me text different contacts to let them know that he was home and safe so they could, in turn, let others know. Rich had nightmares that night, and we got up the next morning, ate breakfast, got ready, and headed out to church. People were so happy to see Rich. They kept coming up, hugging him, and praising God for his safe release. I didn't say much; I just left him to talk and sat by him, holding his hand. The minister announced to the congregation that he was home, and we thanked everyone for their support and prayers. We went home after church, exhausted from all the traveling and the stress of the past two weeks. I felt like I could sleep for days.

Chapter 8

On Monday, I stayed home from work, and Rich and I made an appointment with our family doctor. She told him to come in the next day, and she would see him. Our doctor ordered a battery of tests and set up appointments with some specialists she wanted him to see. She also prescribed the nicotine patch for him. It had worked before when he was trying to quit smoking. I talked to her about some issues I had been having—heart palpitations and panic attacks. I didn't know when they would happen or what triggered the attacks, especially since Rich was home and safe. Panic would just come over my body, sending my heart racing and my scalp tingling. I had never had any before Rich's hostage situation. She recommended that we both see a PTSD counselor. I told her we would see a Christian counseling therapist, and she set up an appointment with one specializing in post-traumatic stress disorder for the following week in a city about an hour away from us. I had plenty of saved personal and sick leave days, so I took off to be home with Rich the first week. I thought it would be good for him and for me to spend some time at home together.

I had talked to all of our sons' teachers. They knew what had happened with my husband and that the boys weren't just skipping school, so they were very good about communicating assignments and giving them time to complete them during the week they were out of school. The other week was Thanksgiving vacation week, so they didn't miss any schoolwork. The boys said they were okay to go back to school, and we thought it would be good to get them back into a routine, so my sister drove them to school. It was a wonderful time, and we began planning for the holidays and decided to have our postponed Thanksgiving dinner that first Saturday after Rich had come home. Darla and Daniel offered to hold

it at their house so we could relax and enjoy time with our family. Rich's family had wanted to come and see him, but he just wanted to take it easy and didn't feel like having a full house.

Even though he was looking forward to resting, Rich wanted to try to get his medical appointments done while I was home with him. His blood work was normal, and he started the nicotine patch to help him quit smoking again. He had a full cardiovascular check-up, too, that came back clear. Our last medical visit for the week was with the counselor. We had decided to meet with her the first time and see what she thought about meeting with us together or separately and how often she thought we should schedule our sessions with her. We drove to McAllen, about an hour to an hour and a half away. We left in plenty of time since we had to find her office, and we didn't know exactly how long that would take, so we got there early. We decided to go into a little café right by the office and have some coffee while we waited for our appointment.

I don't know what I expected of the visit. I had never been to a counselor for treatment except when I went to the one at Rich's rehab center that focused on his issues, and there were a few group sessions about being an enabler. I just knew I really wanted the panic attacks to stop. I would just be sitting in the car or at home, and all of a sudden, my heart started racing, perspiration broke out on my forehead, and I felt a sinking feeling in the pit of my stomach. Whenever it happened, I began praying and trying to breathe slowly and deeply, but the attacks usually lasted at least an hour and came without warning. The doctor greeted us as we neared the door, and she asked us both into her office. "Please have a seat, Mr. and Mrs. Tarpey. Do you mind if I call you Richard and Stephanie?" We answered, "No, please do," as we sat in two comfortable chairs across from her desk. Her office was decorated in calming shades of blue, and she spoke softly but distinctly, putting me at ease. She continued, "I have read your file, Richard, and I know a little of what has occurred, but right now, I want to talk to both of you about what you hope to get out of our sessions, and then I would like to meet with each of you individually to see what we can come up with to help you both."

Rich spoke first. His leg started jumping. He could never keep his right leg still when nervous or uncomfortable. "I was running a crew boat out of Nigeria, and pirates hijacked us. The other captain, the engineer, and I were taken as hostages," he began. "We weren't tortured physically, but our lives were threatened continuously by men that were jacked up on moonshine

and drugs, and we didn't know what was going to happen to us—they shot off guns around our heads and waved their machetes as if they were going to cut off our hands. I am a Christian, and I prayed and prayed for God to protect us and bring us home, but most of all, I prayed for His will to be done, and I knew that if I was killed, I would be in heaven with Him." With tears in my eyes, I said, "The most horrible thing for me was not knowing what was happening to him. I imagined all kinds of horrors. I couldn't sleep. I prayed throughout the days and nights for his safety and God's grace and mercy on the three of them. I almost felt numb after the first days of constant crying. He's home safe, so I don't understand why I have panic attacks and heart palpitations even though God answered our prayers and Rich is back with us. I'm not angry, upset, or fearful when they start, and I didn't have them during the most stressful time of Rich's kidnapping, but now I have them at least once a day, sometimes more."

The doctor explained, "When you are under extreme stress, it raises your adrenaline levels. When the stress doesn't decrease, the levels stay high. Look at my teacup. Just imagine this cup is your body, and the tea in it is adrenaline. Sometimes, your adrenaline is low, sometimes medium, and sometimes high—at the top of the cup. When you are in an extremely stressful, fight-or-flight situation for a long time, your adrenaline levels stay at the top of the cup. Even after the situation has been resolved and your adrenaline has come down some, it is still much closer to the top of the cup because it is your new normal adrenaline level. That means that any small added adrenaline, which can come from excitement, exercise, emotions like fear, anger, or happiness, can push that adrenaline over the top of the cup, causing panic attacks, heart palpitations, dizziness, nausea, and more things people experience when anxious. You have to recognize when that is happening. I will teach you some techniques to lower that adrenaline level until you feel calmer and your physical symptoms decrease."

I had never heard it explained that way, but it really made sense to me—how these physical symptoms of panic could come over me when I wasn't facing an extreme situation. "Will that always happen—how long will it take to bring my adrenaline level down to a normal level?" I wasn't happy with her answer, "Some people never go down to their old normal level. You may be able to even out the adrenaline level at a lower degree than it is now, but it may never be normal for you to have it as low as it was in your past. The important thing is to work on dealing with those symptoms and finding ways to distract your mind from the panic, as well as methods for

calming yourself." Rich said, "We are ready to try whatever you think might help except for medications. We don't want to use antidepressants or sedatives to get through this and then end up unable to stop using them or in a worse state from their side effects." "I agree," I added. The doctor smiled and nodded, "I seldom prescribe any medications when dealing with these situations. Many methods have produced a good outcome for my patients, such as using deep breathing, recognizing what is behind the panic symptoms, and controlling your response to those situations."

She pulled out a white and black electronic gadget. "I am going to connect this clamp to your finger, and it will detect your pulse rate, temperature, and oxygen rate. As you become stressed, you will see the green lights start to turn red." She had my husband place his finger into the clamp connected to the device. As he sat there, she said, "Start thinking of something that happened during your captivity and watch the lights on the device." I watched Rich close his eyes and start thinking and speaking about when he first saw the hijackers swarm onto the boat. The green lights started blinking faster and then turned to red. "Now, I want you to start breathing very deeply. Let your abdomen fill with air and turn your mind to something calming, the ocean waves or the sound of a bird, whatever brings you peace. Slow your deep breaths gradually and let the visualization fill your mind." Rich began breathing deeply and slowly, closing his eyes and relaxing his facial muscles. I could see the red lights dwindling, and the green lights started appearing. "The concept is to recognize what is happening to you when you begin to panic. Sometimes, we don't realize the fear is starting until we are already in full-blown stress mode. This device helps you identify what is going on in your body and focuses you on bringing that stress and adrenaline level down to one your body can handle better. Now, let's hook you up so you can try it, Stephanie."

She unclamped Rich's finger, and I placed mine in the pulse detector. I could see the green lights on the device as they went up, and then I began thinking of my fears for Rich while he was being held in captivity. I thought of not knowing what was happening to him. The green lights quickly turned to red. "Now, think of something peaceful. Find something you can use each time—a happy place." My heart was beating quickly, and I began to turn my mind to a quiet time, imagining when I was pregnant with Ray, and I held our son Rich in my arms as I read him a story before naptime. I began breathing deeply, letting the air fill my stomach and slowing the rate of my breaths. The lights started turning back to green from the

red that had filled the screen. "I will loan you all this one to use, and I will order one for each of you," she said. "It does help to focus your mind on something other than the panic," I agreed. After meeting with us together, the doctor set up a meeting with Rich by himself. We discussed whether she needed to meet with me alone, but I felt we could handle my issues during our group meetings. Rich and I left her office with hope for a more normal future, one where panic and fear did not rule our lives.

Our bodies suffer from the stress and fear we experience throughout our lives. I know that Rich and I brought so much on ourselves through our poor choices and not trusting in God, but some of it has come from outside sources and the actions of other people. As we talked on the drive home, I told Rich that I planned to give my panic to God and that when my heart started palpitating, I would lie down, pray, and meditate on God and His word. He didn't bring us through this traumatic experience to live a life of fear and panic. "For God hath not given us a spirit of fear; but of power, and of love, and of a sound mind" (2 Timothy 1:7 KJV). The pain that we go through, the "monsters" we face, mold us into who we are to become. Jesus Christ endured every emotion that we experience, every pain, and every fear. He overcame them, and He will help us overcome those feelings. As Christians, our desire is to become more like Christ. We learn to have faith and trust God as He brings us through the worst experiences of our lives.

Our postponed Thanksgiving began early on Saturday. I woke up and looked at my husband's face again, just thankful that he was home. After feeding the dogs and cats, I started frying bacon and mixing up the pancakes for breakfast. As usual, the dogs lay at the end of the kitchen tile floor, watching me, hoping I would "accidentally" drop a piece of bacon. They know me well. My husband got up and made coffee. We usually liked to drink it in bed watching the news, but I had too much to do today. Darla and Daniel were hosting our postponed Thanksgiving dinner, and I needed to run to the local HEB grocery store to pick up a few ingredients for some of the dishes we planned to prepare and take over to their house for dinner.

Daniel had been up most of the night smoking a turkey and a ham. Darla was making broccoli and cheese casserole, hot rolls, and stuffing. I made green bean casserole, twice-baked sweet potatoes, and my Uncle's corn casserole dish. Mom and Darla were both making pies. Mom always made her pumpkin pie and a coconut cream pie—Dad's favorite. My sister usually surprised us with pecan pie or a carrot cake. She also made yummy bread puddings with caramel sauce. There would be way too much food.

There always was, but that way, we could all take leftovers home to be enjoyed for days. We always had a lot to be thankful for, but today, I felt especially grateful to have my family around me. We carried our dishes into Darla and Daniel's home as we smelled the familiar aromas of yeast bread baking and smoked turkey wafting through the door.

We overate, of course, and then took a break before dessert. The family moved to the living room and divided into teams for charades. Afterward, we played cards and finally ended with Trivial Pursuit. I think we have played those three games at almost every holiday celebration. I remember playing charades as a child with my mom's family. We have carried over the traditions we loved as children to become part of our children's memories, carving pumpkins, making sugar cookies, family dinners and celebrations, and candlelight Christmas Eve Services. I remember that special Thanksgiving Celebration—a light that shines out from so many family dinners, as the one that we gave thanks to God for my husband's release and safe return to our family.

The PTSD counseling helped me a lot with the panic attacks and also with the stress from my job as a Test Coordinator. The position requires attention to minute details and overseeing hundreds of teachers who serve as test administrators, training them, assigning their test sites, getting the correct documents ready, and organizing thousands of students throughout the year for state and national tests. One wrong step, one wrong test, and you can negatively impact a student's future, college admittance, and scholarship possibilities. When I returned to work, I had to step right back into organizing our school for the spring state testing and training the test administrators. It requires many hours of intense documentation. Rich was home throughout the day and continued working on recovering from his experience. Outside of work, we attended the boys' sports activities, basketball games, and golf tournaments. Rich didn't get to be there for our sons' sports throughout the years as much because he was often at work. When he was home, he was always there. We focused on our family time together and getting Rich healthy.

Life continued on. Rich and I worked with the counselor and God and learned how to manage the panic attacks resulting from the stress and anxiety over his kidnapping and captivity. Over the years, some people have asked me how much money Rich's company gave us because he was kidnapped while on the job. I would look at them and reply, "Why would we ask them for money—they paid hundreds of thousands of dollars to bring my husband

CHAPTER 8

home safe, and men risked their lives to deliver the ransom to dangerous men who would kill them if they had the chance and take the money anyway. They paid us with my husband's life—what price is that worth?" It always stunned me anytime someone questioned me about that—I didn't understand why people thought we would try to make money off of a company that had already paid so much and was successful in rescuing their men. We were just grateful to God that Rich was brought home safely.

After being home and undergoing PTSD counseling for about three months, Rich felt ready to return to work. His company asked him where he would like to captain a crew boat since they operated in several areas, including South America. We talked it over. I really wanted him to stay closer to home, and he was leery of going overseas again, so he requested the Gulf of Mexico. He went back to work in the middle of March after the boys' spring break. It was a big step for the family, but since he had worked in the Gulf before with a different company, we felt comfortable with it. I was nervous about him leaving, but I realized that he needed to continue in his career and that it would be good for him to face any fears he might have by getting back into captaining. We settled into a routine with his new schedule of one month on the boat and two weeks home. The boys and I focused on work, school, and their activities. We kept busy, and I could talk to Rich anytime since he was in range. I still had panic attack episodes, but I used the strategies the counselor taught me to calm down, and the boys each had the opportunity to speak with counselors at their schools.

In late October, I began to feel a lot of anxiety and increased heart palpitations. I had moved from the position of testing coordinator at the high school to librarian, and it was a lot less stressful, so I didn't understand why I was feeling so anxious. I talked to Rich about it, and he said he had been feeling that way, too. Finally, after our discussions, we realized it was because we were coming up on the year anniversary of his kidnapping. Knowing the reason for the anxiety helped me to deal with it better. Even now, though, after all these years, I still feel anxiety as autumn approaches, the time of year when he was taken and held hostage.

Chapter 9

I have set down to write this story so many times. It has been challenging because, every time, I start having panic attacks and nightmares about the events. Our lives have changed in many ways. Our sons have grown up and are beginning their lives in new places. My husband is now running tugs in Alaska instead of crew boats in the Gulf of Mexico. We have lost dear loved ones. We are definitely at a better place in our relationship with God. He is the focus of our lives. We also make more time for each other and our families, even when we have to travel to do it. We have learned to live in the moment, and when fear or anxiety tries to take over our minds, we remember what God has done for us. He has brought our family out of darkness, and His faithfulness will see us through to the end.

AF251475